THE BEAUTIFUL
NECESSITY

THE BEAUTIFUL NECESSITY

Seven Essays on
Theosophy and Architecture

by
CLAUDE BRAGDON

ROCHESTER, N. Y.
THE MANAS PRESS
1910

*Copyright 1910
by*
Claude Bragdon

"Let us build altars to the Beautiful Necessity"
—Emerson

CONTENTS

I
THE THEOSOPHIC VIEW OF THE ART OF ARCHITECTURE   9 - 21

II
UNITY AND POLARITY . . . . . . 22 - 32

III
CHANGELESS CHANGE . . . . . . 33 - 49

IV
THE BODILY TEMPLE . . . . . . 50 - 59

V
LATENT GEOMETRY . . . . . . 60 - 75

VI
THE ARITHMETIC OF BEAUTY . . . . . 76 - 84

VII
FROZEN MUSIC . . . . 85 - 92

CONCLUSION 93

I

THE THEOSOPHIC VIEW OF THE ART OF ARCHITECTURE

ONE of the many advantages of a thorough assimilation of what may be called the theosophic idea is that it can be applied with advantage to every department of knowledge and of human activity: like the key to a cryptogram, it renders clear and simple that which before was intricate and obscure. Let us apply this key to the subject of art, and to the art of architecture in particular, and let us see if by so doing we may not learn more of art than we knew before, and more of theosophy, too.

The theosophic idea is that everything is an expression of the Self,—or whatever other name one may choose to give to that immanent unknown reality which forever hides behind all phenomenal life,—but because on the physical plane our only avenue of knowledge is sense perception, a more exact expression of the theosophic idea would be: Everything is the expression of the Self in terms of sense. Art, accordingly, is the expression of the Self in terms of sense. Now, though the Self is one, sense is not one, but manifold, and so there are arts, each addressed to some particular faculty or group of faculties, and each expressing some particular quality or group of qualities of the Self. The white light of Truth is thus broken up into a rainbow-tinted spectrum of Beauty, in which the various arts are colors, each distinct, yet merging one into another,—poetry into music; painting into decoration; decoration becoming sculpture; sculpture, architecture, and so on.

In such a spectrum of the arts each one occupies a definite place, and all together form a series of which music and architecture are the two extremes. That such is their relative position may be demonstrated in various ways: the theosophic explanation involving the familiar idea of the "pairs of opposites" would be something as follows: According to the Hindu-Aryan theory, Brahma, that the world might be born, fell asunder into man and wife, became in other words, *name and form.** The two universal aspects of name and form are what philosophers call the two "modes of consciousness," one of time, and the other of space. These are the two gates through which ideas enter phenomenal life: the two boxes, as it were, that contain all the toys with which we play. Everything, if we were only keen enough to perceive it, bears the mark of one or the other of them, and may be classified accordingly. In such a classification music is seen to be allied to time, and architecture to space, because music is successive in its mode of manifestation, and in time alone everything would occur successively, one thing following another; while architecture, on the other hand, impresses itself upon the beholder all at once, and in space alone all things would exist simultaneously. Music, which is in time alone, without any relation to space, and architecture, which is in space alone, without any relation to time, are thus seen to stand at opposite ends of the art spectrum, and to be, in a sense, the only "pure" arts, because in all the others the elements of both time and space enter in varying proportions, either actually or by implication. Poetry and the drama are allied to music insomuch as the ideas and images of which they are made up are presented successively, yet these images are, for the most part, forms of space. Sculpture, on the other hand, is clearly allied to architecture, and so to space, but the element of *action,* suspended though it be, affiliates it with the opposite, or time pole. Painting occupies a middle position, since in it space instead of being actual has become ideal,—three dimensions being expressed through the mediumship of two,—and time enters into it more largely than into sculpture by reason of the greater ease with which complicated action can be indicated: a picture being nearly always time arrested in mid-course, a moment transfixed.

In order to form a just conception of the relation between music and architecture it is necessary that the two should be conceived of, not as standing at opposite ends of a series represented by a straight line, but rather in

---

*The quaint Oriental imagery here employed should not blind the reader to the precise scientific accuracy of the idea of which this imagery is the vehicle. Schopenhauer says: "Polarity, or the sundering of a force into two quantitatively different and opposed activities, striving after re-union, . . . is a fundamental type of almost all the phenomena of nature, from the magnet and the crystal to man himself."

juxtaposition, as in the ancient Egyptian symbol of a serpent holding its tail in its mouth, the head in this case corresponding to music, and the tail to architecture; in other words, though in one sense they are the most widely separated of the arts, in another they are the most closely related.

Music being purely in time and architecture being purely in space, each is, in a manner, and to a degree not possible with any of the other arts, convertible into the other, by reason of the correspondence subsisting between intervals of time and intervals of space. A perception of this may have inspired the famous saying that architecture is *frozen music,* a poetical statement of a philosophical truth, since that which in music is expressed by means of harmonious intervals of time and pitch, successively, after the manner of time, may be translated into corresponding intervals of architectural void and solid, height and width.

In another sense music and architecture are allied. They alone of all the arts are purely creative, since in them is presented, not a likeness of some known idea, but *a thing-in-itself* brought to a distinct and complete expression of its nature. Neither a musical composition nor a work of architecture depends for its effectiveness upon resemblances to natural sounds in the one case, or to natural forms in the other. Of none of the other arts is this to such a degree true: they are not so much creative as re-creative, for in them all the artist takes his subject ready made from nature and presents it anew according to the dictates of his genius.

The characteristic differences between music and architecture are the same as those which subsist between time and space. Now time and space are such abstract ideas that they can be best understood through their corresponding correlatives in the natural world, for it is a fundamental theosophic tenet that nature everywhere abounds in such correspondences; that nature, in its myriad forms, is indeed the concrete presentment of abstract unities. The energy which everywhere informs matter is a type of time within space; the mind working in and through the body is another expression of the same thing. Accordingly, music is dynamic, subjective, mental, of one dimension; while architecture is static, objective, physical, of three dimensions; sustaining the same relation to music and the other arts as does the human body to the various organs which compose, and consciousnesses which animate it, (it being the reservatory of these organs and the vehicle of these consciousnesses); and a work of architecture, in like manner, may, and sometimes does include all of the other arts within itself. Sculpture accentuates and enriches, painting adorns it, works of literature are stored within it, poetry and the drama awake its echoes, while music thrills to its uttermost recesses, like the very spirit of life tingling through the body's fibres.

Such being the relation between them, the difference in the nature of the ideas bodied forth in music and in architecture becomes readily apparent. Music is interior, abstract, subjective, speaking directly to the soul in a simple and universal language whose meaning is made personal and particular in the breast of each listener: "Music alone of all arts," says Balzac, "has power to make us live within ourselves." A work of architecture is the exact opposite of this; existing principally and primarily for the uses of the body, it is, like the body, a concrete organism, attaining to esthetic expression only in the reconciliation and fulfilment of many conflicting practical requirements. Music is pure beauty, the voice of the unfettered and perpetually evanishing soul of things; architecture is that soul imprisoned in a form, become subject to the law of casualty, beaten upon by the elements, at war with gravity, the slave of man. One is the Ariel of the arts, the other, Caliban.

Coming now to the consideration of architecture in its historical rather than in its philosophical aspect, it will be shown how certain theosophical concepts are applicable here. Of these none is more familiar and none more fundamental than the idea of reincarnation. By reincarnation more than mere physical re-birth is implied, for physical re-birth is but a single manifestation of that universal law of alternation of state, of animation of vehicles, and progression through successive planes, in accordance with which all things move, and as it were make music,—each cycle complete, yet part of a larger cycle, the incarnate monad passing through correlated changes, carrying along and bringing into manifestation in each higher arc of the spiral the experience accumulated in all preceding states, and at the same time unfolding that power of the Self peculiar to the plane in which it happens to be manifesting.

This law finds exemplification in the history of architecture in the orderly flow of the building impulse from one nation and one country to a different nation and a different country: its new vehicle of manifestation; also in the continuity and increasing complexity of the development of that impulse in manifestation; each "incarnation" summarizing all those which have gone before, and adding some new factor peculiar to itself alone; each being a growth, a life, with periods corresponding to childhood, youth, maturity and decadence; each also typifying in its entirety some single one of these life periods, and revealing some special aspect or power of the Self.

For the sake of clearness and brevity the consideration of only one of several architectural evolutions will be attempted: that which, arising in the north of Africa, spread to southern Europe, thence to the northwest of Europe and to England; the architecture, in short, of what is popularly known as the civilized world.

This architecture, anterior to the Christian era, may be broadly divided into three great periods, during which it was successively practiced by three peoples: the Egyptians, the Greeks, and the Romans. Then intervened the Dark Ages, and a new art arose, the Gothic, which was a flowering out in stone of the spirit of Christianity. This was in turn succeeded by the Renaissance, the impulse of which remains to-day unexhausted. In each of these architectures the peculiar genius of a people and of a period attained to a beautiful, complete, and coherent utterance, and notwithstanding the considerable intervals of time which sometimes separated them, they succeeded one another logically and inevitably, and each was related to the one which preceded and which followed it in a particular and intimate manner.

The power and wisdom of ancient Egypt was vested in its priesthood, which was composed of individuals exceptionally qualified by birth and training for their high office, tried by the severest ordeals and bound by the most solemn oaths. The priests were honored and privileged above all other men, and spent their lives dwelling apart from the multitude in vast and magnificent temples, dedicating themselves to the study and practice of religion, philosophy, science, and art,—subjects then intimately related, not widely separated as they are now. These men were the architects of ancient Egypt; theirs, the minds which directed the hands that built those time-defying monuments.

The rites which the priests practiced centered about what are known as the Lesser and the Greater Mysteries. These consisted of representations, by means of symbol and allegory, under conditions and amid surroundings the most awe-inspiring, of those great truths concerning man's nature, origin, and destiny, of which the priests—in reality a brotherhood of initiates and their pupils—were the custodians. These ceremonies were made the occasion for the initiation of neophytes into the order, and the advancement of the already initiated into its successive degrees. For the practice of such rites, and others, designed to impress not the elect, but the multitude, the great temples of Egypt were constructed. Everything about them was calculated to induce a deep seriousness of mind, and to inspire feelings of awe, dread, and even terror, so as to test the candidate's fortitude of soul to the utmost.

The avenue of approach to an Egyptian temple was flanked on either side, sometimes for a mile or more, with great stone sphinxes, that emblem of man's dual nature, the god emerging from the beast. The entrance was through a single high doorway between two towering pylons, presenting a vast surface sculptured and painted over with many strange and enigmatic figures and flanked by aspiring obelisks, and seated colossi with faces austere and calm. The large court thus entered was surrounded by high walls and colonnades, but was open to the sky. Opposite the first doorway was another, admitting to a somewhat smaller enclosure, a forest of enormous carved and painted columns supporting a roof through the apertures of which sunshine gleamed, or dim light filtered down. Beyond this, in turn, were other courts and apartments culminating in some inmost sacred sanctuary.

Not alone in their temples, but in their tombs and pyramids, and all the sculptured monuments of the Egyptians, there is the same insistence upon the sublimity, mystery, and awfulness of life, which they seem to have felt so profoundly. But more than this, the conscious thought of the masters who conceived them, the buildings of Egypt give utterance also to the agony and toil of the thousands of slaves and captives which hewed the stones out of the heart of the rock, dragged them long distances, and placed them one upon another, so that these buildings oppress while they inspire, for there is in them no freedom, no spontaneity, no individuality, but everywhere the felt presence of an iron conventionality, of a stern, immutable law.

In Egyptian architecture is symbolized the condition of the human soul awakened from its long sleep in nature, and become conscious at once of its divine source and of the leaden burden of its fleshly envelope. Egypt is humanity new born, bound still with an umbilical cord to nature, and strong not so much with its own strength as with the strength of its mother. This idea is aptly typified in those gigantic colossi flanking the entrance to some rock-cut temple, which though entire are yet part of the living cliff out of which they were fashioned.

In the architecture of Greece the note of dread and mystery yields to one of pure joyousness and freedom. The terrors of childhood have been outgrown, and man revels in the indulgence of his unjaded appetites and in the exercise of his awakened reasoning faculties. In Greek art is preserved that evanescent beauty of youth which, coming but once and continuing but for a short interval in every human life, is yet that for which all antecedent states seem a preparation, and of which all subsequent ones are in some sort an effect. Greece typifies adolescence, the love age, and so throughout the centuries humanity has turned to the contemplation of her just as a man all his life long secretly cherishes the memory of his first love.

An impassioned sense of beauty and an enlightened reason characterize the productions of Greek architecture during its best period. The perfection then attained was possible only in a nation whereof the citizens were themselves critics and amateurs of art, one wherein the artist was honored and his work appreciated in all its beauty and subtlety. The Greek architect was less bound by tradition and precedent than was the Egyptian, and he worked unhampered by any restrictions, save such as, like the laws of harmony in music, helped rather than hindered his genius to express itself,— restrictions founded on sound reason, the value of which had been proved by experience.

The Doric order was employed for all large temples, since it possessed in fullest measure the qualities of simplicity and dignity, the attributes appropriate to greatness. Quite properly, also, its formulas were more fixed than those of any other style. The Ionic order, the feminine of which the Doric may be considered the corresponding masculine, was employed for smaller temples; like a woman, it was more supple and adaptable than the Doric, its proportions were more slender and graceful, its lines more flowing, and its ornament more delicate and profuse. A freer and more elaborate style than either of these, infinitely various, seeming to obey no law save that of beauty, was used sometimes for small monuments and temples, such as the Tower of the Winds, and the monument of Lysicrates at Athens.

Because the Greek architect was at liberty to improve upon the work of his predecessors if he could, no temple was just like any other, and they form an ascending scale of excellence, culminating in the Acropolis group. Every detail was considered not only with relation to its position and function, but in regard to its intrinsic beauty as well, so that the merest fragment, detached from the building of which it formed a part, is found worthy of being treasured in our museums for its own sake.

Just as every detail of a Greek temple was adjusted to its position and expressed its office, so the building itself was made to fit its site and to show

1

forth its purpose, forming with the surrounding buildings a unit of a larger whole. The Athenian Acropolis is an illustration of this: it is an irregular fortified hill, bearing diverse monuments in various styles, at unequal levels and at different angles with one another, yet the whole arrangement seems as organic and inevitable as the disposition of the features of a face. The Acropolis is an example of the ideal Architectural Republic wherein each individual contributes to the welfare of all, and at the same time enjoys the utmost personal liberty (Illustration 1).

Very different is the spirit bodied forth in the architecture of Imperial Rome. The iron hand of its sovereignty, encased within the silken glove of its luxury, finds its prototype in buildings which were stupendous crude brute masses of brick and concrete, hidden within a covering of rich marbles and mosaics, wrought in beautiful, but often meaningless forms by clever, degenerate Greeks. The genius of Rome finds its most characteristic expression, not in temples to the high gods, but rather in those vast and complicated structures—basilicas, amphitheatres, baths—built for the amusement and purely temporal needs of the people.

If Egypt typifies the childhood of the race and Greece its beautiful youth, Republican Rome represents its strong manhood,—a soldier filled with the lust of war and the love of glory,—and Imperial Rome its degeneracy: that soldier become conqueror, decked out in plundered finery and sunk in sensuality, tolerant of all who minister to his pleasures but terrible to all who interfere with them.

The fall of Rome marked the end of the ancient Pagan world. Above its ruin Christian civilization in the course of time arose. Gothic architecture is an expression of the Christian spirit; in it is manifest the reaction from licentiousness to asceticism. Man's spiritual nature, awakening in a body worn and weakened by debaucheries, longs ardently and tries vainly to escape. Of some such mood a Gothic cathedral is the expression; its vaulting, marvelously supported upon slender shafts by reason of a nicely adjusted equilibrium of forces; its restless, upward-reaching pinnacles and spires; its ornament, intricate and enigmatic; all these suggest the over-strained organism of an ascetic; while its vast, shadowy interior, lit by marvelously traceried and jeweled windows which hold the eyes in a hypnotic thrall, is like his soul: filled with world sadness, dead to the bright, brief joys of sense, seeing only heavenly visions, knowing none but mystic raptures.

Thus it is that the history of architecture illustrates and enforces the theosophical teaching that everything of man's creating is made in his own image. Architecture mirrors the life of the individual and of the race, which is the life of the individual written large in time and space. The terrors of childhood; the keen interests and appetites of youth; the strong, stern joy of conflict which comes with manhood; the lust, the greed, the cruelty of a materialized old age,—all these serve but as a preparation for the life of the spirit, in which the man becomes again as a little child, going over the whole round, but on a higher arc of the spiral.

The final, or fourth state being only in some sort a repetition of the first, it would be reasonable to look for a certain correspondence between Egyptian and Gothic architecture, and such a correspondence there is, though it is more easily divined than demonstrated. In both there is the same deeply religious spirit; both convey, in some obscure yet potent manner, a sense of the soul being near the surface of life. There is the same love of mystery and of symbolism; and in both may be observed the tendency to create strange, composite figures to typify transcendental ideas, the sphinx seeming a blood brother to the gargoyle. The conditions under which each architecture flourished were not dissimilar, for each was formulated and controlled by small, well organized bodies of sincerely religious and highly enlightened men—the priesthood in the one case, the masonic guilds in the other—working together towards the consummation of great undertakings amid a populace for the most part oblivious of the profound and subtle meanings of which their work was full. In Mediæval Europe, as in ancient Egypt, fragments of the Secret Doctrine—transmitted in the symbols and secrets of the cathedral builders—determined much of Gothic architecture.

The architecture of the Renaissance period, which succeeded the Gothic, corresponds again, in the spirit, which animates it, to Greek architecture, which succeeded the Egyptian; for the Renaissance, as the name implies, was nothing other than an attempt to revive Classical antiquity. Scholars writing in what they conceived to be a Classical style, sculptors modeling Pagan deities, and architects building according to their understanding of Vitruvian methods, succeeded in producing works like, yet different from the originals they followed,—different because, animated by a spirit unknown to the ancients, they embodied a new ideal.

In all the productions of the early Renaissance, "that first transcendent springtide of the modern world," there is that evanescent grace and beauty of youth which was seen to have pervaded Greek art, but it is a grace and beauty of a different sort. The Greek artist sought to attain to a certain abstract perfection of type; to build a temple which should combine all the excellencies of every similar temple, to carve a figure impersonal in the highest sense, which should embody every beauty. The artist of the Renaissance, on the other hand, delighted not so much in the type as in the variation from it. Preoccupied with the unique mystery of the individual soul—a sense of which was Christianity's gift to Christendom—he endeavored to portray that wherein a particular person is unique and singular. Acutely conscious also of his own individuality, instead of effacing it, he made his work the vehicle and expression of that individuality. The history of Renaissance architecture, as Symonds has pointed out, is the history of a few eminent individuals, each one moulding and modifying the style in a manner peculiar to himself alone. In the hands of Brunelleschi it was stern and powerful; Bramante made it chaste, elegant and graceful; Palladio made it formal, cold, symmetrical; while with Sansovino and Sammichele it became sumptuous and bombastic.

As the Renaissance ripened to its decay, architecture assumed more and more the characteristics which distinguished that of Rome during the decadence. In both there is the same lack of simplicity and sincerity, the same profusion of debased and meaningless ornament, and there is an increasing disposition to conceal and falsify the construction by surface decoration.

The final part of this second, or modern architectural cycle lies still in the future. It is not unreasonable to believe that the movement towards mysticism, of which modern theosophy is a phase and the spiritualization of science an episode, will flower out into an architecture which will be in some sort a reincarnation of and a return to the Gothic spirit, employing new materials, new methods, and developing new forms to show forth ancient verities.

In studying these salient periods in the history of European architecture, it is possible to trace a gradual growth or unfolding, as of a plant. It is a fact fairly well established that the Greeks derived their architecture and ornament from Egypt. The Romans in turn borrowed from the Greeks, while a Gothic cathedral is a lineal descendant from a Roman basilica.

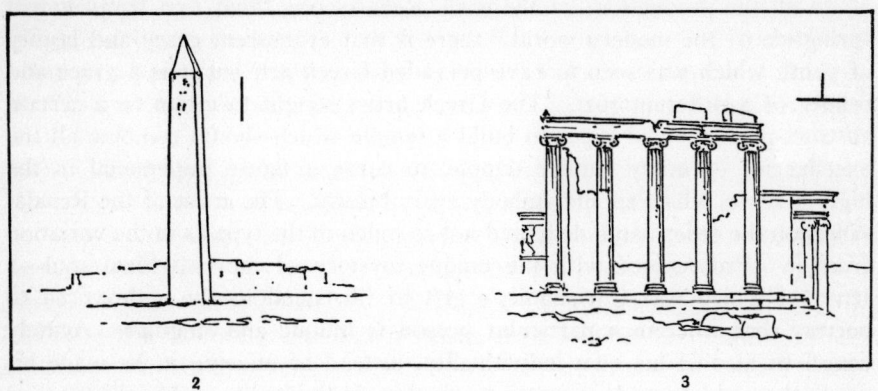

The Egyptians, in their constructions, did little more than to place enormous stones on end, and pile one huge block upon another. They used many columns placed close together. The spaces which they spanned were inconsiderable. The upright, or supporting member may be said to have been in Egyptian architecture the predominant one. A vertical line, therefore, may be taken as the simplest and most abstract symbol of Egyptian architecture (Illustration 2). It remained for the Greeks fully to develop the lintel. In their architecture the vertical member, or column, existed solely for the sake of the horizontal member, or lintel; it rarely stood alone, as in the case of an Egyptian obelisk. The columns of the Greek temples were

reduced to those proportions most consistent with strength and beauty, and the intercolumnations were relatively greater than in Egyptian examples. It may truly be said that Greek architecture exhibits the perfect equality and equipoise of vertical and horizontal elements and these only, no other factor entering in. Its graphic symbol would therefore be composed of a vertical and a horizontal line (Illustration 3). The Romans, while retaining the column and lintel of the Greeks, deprived them of their structural significance and subordinated them to the semi-circular arch, and the semi-cylindrical and hemispherical vault, the truly characteristic and determining forms of Roman architecture. Our symbol grows, therefore, by the addition of the arc of a circle (Illustration 4). In Gothic architecture, column, lintel, arch and vault are all retained in changed form, but that which more than anything else differentiates Gothic architecture from any style which preceded it, is the introduction of the principle of an equilibrium of forces, of a state of balance rather than a state of rest, arrived at by the opposition of one thrust with another contrary to it. This fact can be indicated graphically by two opposing inclined lines, and these united to the preceding symbol yield an accurate abstract of the elements of Gothic architecture (Illustration 5).

All this is but an unusual application of a familiar theosophic teaching, namely, that it is the method of nature on every plane and in every department not to omit anything that has gone before, but to store it up and carry it along and bring it into manifestation later. Nature everywhere proceeds like the jingle of *The House that Jack Built:* she repeats each time all she has learned, and adds another line for subsequent repetition.

II

UNITY AND POLARITY

THEOSOPHY, both as a doctrine, or system of thought which discovers correlations between things apparently unrelated, and as a life, or system of training whereby it is possible to gain the power to perceive and use these correlations for worthy ends, is of great value to the creative artist, whose success depends on the extent to which he works organically, conforming to the cosmic pattern, proceeding rationally and rhythmically to some predetermined end. It is of value, no less, to the layman, the critic, the art amateur—to anyone, in fact, who would come to an accurate and intimate understanding and appreciation of every variety of aesthetic endeavor. For the benefit of such I shall try to trace some of those correlations which theosophy affirms, and indicate their bearing upon art, and upon the art of architecture in particular.

One of the things which theosophy teaches is that those transcendent glimpses of a divine order and harmony throughout the universe vouchsafed the poet and the mystic in their moments of vision are not the paradoxes— the paronomasia, as it were—of an intoxicated state of consciousness, but glimpses of reality. We are all of us participators in a world of concrete music, geometry and number,—a world, that is, of sounds, odors, forms, motions, colors, so mathematically related and co-ordinated that our pigmy bodies, equally with the farthest star, vibrate to the music of the spheres. There is a *Beautiful Necessity* which rules the world, which is a law of nature and equally a law of art, for art is idealized creation: nature carried to a higher power by reason of its passage through a human consciousness. Thought and emotion tend to crystallize into forms of beauty as inevitably as does the frost on a window pane. Art, therefore, in one of its aspects, is the weaving of a pattern, the communication of an order and a method to the material or medium employed. Although no masterpiece was ever created by the conscious following of set rules, for the true artist works unconsciously, instinctively, as the bird sings, or as the bee builds its honey-cell, yet an analysis of any masterpiece reveals the fact that its author (like the bird and the bee) has "followed the rules without knowing them."

Helmholtz says, "No doubt is now entertained that beauty is subject to laws and rules dependent on the nature of human intelligence. The difficulty consists in the fact that these laws and rules, on whose fulfilment beauty depends, are not consciously present in the mind of the artist who creates the work, or of the observer who contemplates it." Nevertheless they are discoverable, and can be formulated, after a fashion. We have only to read aright the lesson of the Good Law everywhere portrayed in the vast picture-book of nature and of art.

The first truth therein published is the law of Unity—oneness; for there is one Self, one Life, which, myriad in manifestation, is yet in essence ever one. Atom and universe, man and the world, each is a unit, an organic and coherent whole. The application of this law to art is so obvious as to be almost unnecessary of elucidation, for to say that a work of art must possess unity, must seem to proceed from a single impulse and be the embodiment of one dominant idea, is to state a truism. In a work of architecture the co-ordination of its various parts with one another is almost the measure of its success. We remember any masterpiece—the cathedral of Paris no less than the pyramids of Egypt—by the singleness of its appeal; complex it may be, but it is a co-ordinated complexity; variety it may possess, but it is a variety in an all-embracing unity.

The second law, not contradicting, but supplementing the first, is the law of Polarity, i. e., duality. All things have sex, are either masculine or feminine. This, too, is the reflection, on a lower plane, of one of those transcendental truths taught by the Ancient Wisdom, namely that the Logos, in His voluntarily circumscribing His infinite life in order that He might manifest, incloses himself within his limiting veil, Maya, and that His Life appears as Spirit (male) and his Maya as Matter (female), the two being never disjointed during manifestation. The two terms of this polarity are endlessly repeated throughout nature: in sun and moon, day and night, fire and water, man and woman—and so on. A close inter-relation is always discerned to subsist between corresponding members of such pairs of opposites: sun, day, fire, man, express and embody the primal and active aspect of the manifesting deity; moon, night, water, woman, its secondary and passive. Moreover, each in a sense implies, or brings to mind, the others of its class: man, like the sun is lord of day, a direct and devastating force like fire; woman is subject to the lunar rhythm; like water, she is soft, sinuous, fecund.

The part which this polarity plays in the arts is important, and the constant and characteristic distinction between the two terms is a thing far beyond mere contrast.

In music they are the major and the minor modes: the typical, or representative chords of the dominant seventh and of the tonic (the two chords into which Schopenhauer affirms all music can be resolved), a partial dissonance and a consonance, a chord of suspense and a chord of satisfaction. In speech the two are vowel and consonant sounds, the type of the first being *a,* a sound of suspense, made with the mouth open, and of the second *m,* a sound of satisfaction, made by closing the mouth; their combination forms the sacred syllable Om. In painting they are warm colors and cold, the pole of the first being in red, the color of fire, which excites, and of the second in blue, the color of water, which calms; in the arts of design they are lines straight (like fire), and flowing (like water); masses light (like the day), and dark (like night). In architecture they are the column, or supporting member, which resists the force of gravity, and the horizontal member, or lintel, which succumbs to it; they are vertical lines, which are aspiring, effortful, and horizontal lines, which are restful to the eye and mind.

It is desirable to have an instant and keen realization of this sex quality, and to make this easier, some sort of a classification and analysis must be attempted. Those things which are allied to, and partake of the nature of *time* are masculine, and those which are allied to and partake of the nature of *space* are feminine, as motion and matter, mind and body, etc. The English words "masculine" and "feminine" are too intimately associated with the idea of physical sex properly to designate the terms of this polarity. In Japanese philosophy and art the two are called In and Yo (In, feminine; Yo, masculine), and these little words, being free from the limitations of their English correlatives, will be found convenient, Yo to designate that which is simple, direct, primary, active, positive; and In, that which is complex, indirect, derivative, passive, negative. Things hard, straight, fixed,

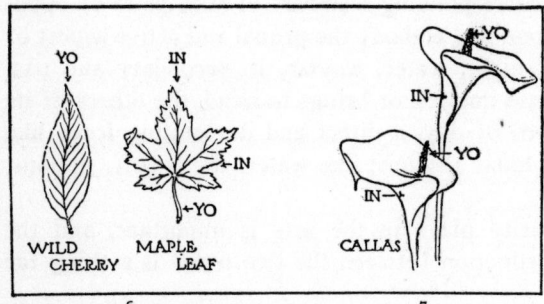

vertical are Yo; things soft, curved, horizontal, fluctuating are In, and so on.

In passing it may be said that the superiority of the line, mass, and color composition of Japanese prints and kakemonos to that exhibited in the vastly more pretentious easel pictures of modern Occidental artists—a superiority now generally acknowledged by connoisseurs—is largely due to the conscious following, on the part of the Japanese, of this principle of sex-complementaries.

Nowhere are In and Yo more simply and adequately imaged than in the vegetable kingdom. The trunk of a tree is Yo, its foliage, In; and in each stem and leaf the two are repeated. A calla, consisting of a single straight and rigid spadix embraced by a soft and tenderly curved spathe, affords an almost perfect expression of the characteristic differences between Yo and In and their reciprocal relation to each other. The two are not often combined in such simplicity and perfection in a single form. The straight, vertical reeds which so often grow in still, shallow water, find their complement in the curved lily-pads which lie horizontally on its surface. Trees such as the pine and hemlock, which are excurrent—those in which the branches start successively (i. e., after the manner of time) from a straight and vertical central stem—are Yo; trees such as the elm and willow, which are deliquescent,—those in which the trunk dissolves, as it were, simultaneously (after the manner of space) into its branches, are In. All tree forms lie in or between these two extremes, and leaves are susceptible of a similar classification. It will be seen to be a classification according to time and space, for the characteristic of time is *succession,* and of space *simultaneousness;* the first is expressed symbolically by elements arranged with relation to axial lines; the second, by elements arranged with relation to focal points (Illustrations 6, 7).

The art student should train himself to recognize In and Yo in all their Protean presentments throughout nature,—in the cloud upon the mountain, the wave against the cliff, in the tracery of trees against the sky,—that he may the more readily recognize them in his chosen art, whatever that art may be. If it happens to be painting, he will endeavor to discern this law of duality in the composition of every masterpiece, recognizing an instinctive obedience to it in that favorite device of the great Renaissance masters of making an architectural setting for their groups of figures, and he will delight to trace the law in all its ramifications of contrast between complementaries in line, color and mass (Illustration 8).

With reference to architecture, as a general proposition it is true that architectural forms have been developed through necessity, the function seeking and finding its appropriate form. For example, the buttress of a Gothic cathedral was developed by the necessity of resisting the thrust of the interior vaulting without encroaching upon the nave; the main lines of a buttress conform to the direction of the thrust, and the pinnacle with which it terminates is a logical shape for the masonry necessary to hold the top in position (Illustration 9). Research along these lines is very interesting and fruitful of result, but there remains a certain number of architectural forms whose origin cannot be explained in any such manner. The secret of their undying charm lies in the fact that in them In and Yo stand symbolized and contrasted. They no longer obey a law of utility, but an abstract law of beauty, for in becoming sexually expressive, as it were, the construction itself is sometimes weakened or falsified. The familiar classic console or modillion is an example: although in general contour it is well adapted to its function as a supporting bracket, embedded in, and projecting from a wall, yet the scroll-like ornament with which its sides

CLEOPATRA MELTING THE PEARL, BY TIEPOLO

8

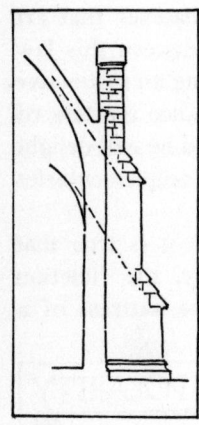

are embellished gives it the appearance of not entering the wall at all, but of being stuck against it in some miraculous manner. This defect in functional expressiveness is more than compensated for by the perfection with which feminine and masculine characteristics are expressed and contrasted in the exquisite double spiral, opposed to the straight lines of the moulding which it subtends (Illustration 10). Again, by fluting the shaft of a column its area of cross-section is diminished but the appearance of strength is enhanced, because its masculine character—as a supporting member resisting the force of gravity—is emphasized.

The importance of the so-called "orders" lies in the fact that they are architecture epitomized, as it were. A building consists of a wall upholding a roof: support and weight; the type of the first is the column, which may be conceived of as a condensed section of wall, and of the second the lintel, which may be conceived of as a condensed section of roof. The column, being vertical, is Yo; the lintel, being horizontal, is In. To mark an entablature with horizontal lines in the form of mouldings, and the columns with vertical lines in the form of flutes, as is done in all the so-called Classic Orders, is a gain in functional and sex expressiveness, and consequently in art (Illustration 11).

The column is again divided into the shaft, which is Yo, and the capital, which is In. The capital is itself twofold, consisting of a curved member and an angular member. These two appear in their utmost simplicity in the echinus (In), and the abacus (Yo) of a Greek Doric cap. The former was adorned with painted leaf forms, characteristically feminine, and the latter with the angular fret and meander (Illustration 12). The Ionic capital, belonging

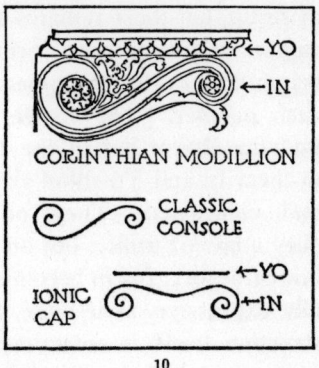

to a more feminine style, exhibits the abacus subordinated to that beautiful cushion-shaped member with its two spirally marked volutes. This, though a less rational and expressive form for its particular office than is the echinus of the Doric cap, is a far more perfect symbol of the feminine element in

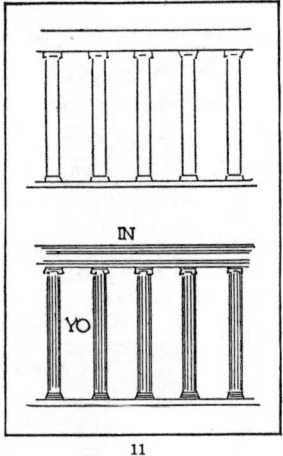

11

nature. There is an essential identity between the Ionic cap and the Classic console before referred to, although superficially the two do not resemble one another, as a straight line and a double spiral are elements common to both (Illustration 10). The Corinthian capital consists of an ordered mass of delicately sculptured leaf and scroll forms sustaining an abacus which, though relatively masculine, is yet more curved and feminine than that of any other style. In the caulicole of a Corinthian cap In and Yo are again contrasted. In the unique and exquisite capital from the Tower of the Winds, at Athens, the two are well suggested in the simple, erect, and pointed leaf forms of the upper part, contrasted with the complex, deliquescent, rounded ones from which they spring. The essential identity of principle subsisting between this cap and the Renaissance baluster by San Gallo is apparent (Illustration 13).

This law of sex-expressiveness is of such universality that it can be made the basis of an analysis of the architectural ornament of any style or period. It is more than mere opposition and contrast. The egg and tongue motif, which has persisted throughout so many centuries and survived so many styles, exhibits an alternation of forms resembling phallic emblems. Yo and In are well suggested in the channel triglyphs and the sculptured metopes of a Doric frieze, in the straight and vertical mullions and the flowing tracery of Gothic windows, in the banded torus, the bead and reel, and other familiar ornamented mouldings (Illustrations 14, 15, 16).

There are indications that at some time during the development of Gothic architecture in

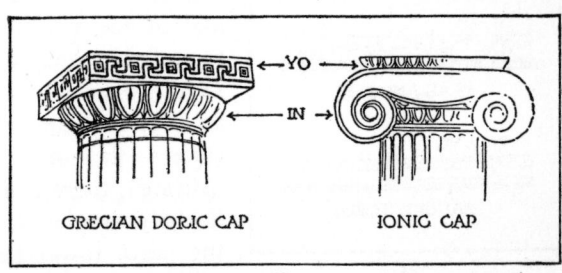

12

France, this sex-distinction became a recognized principle, moulding and modifying the design of a cathedral in much the same way that sex modifies bodily structure. The masonic guilds of the Middle Ages were custodians of the esoteric—which is the theosophic—side of the Christian faith, and every student of the Secret Doctrine knows how fundamental and far-reaching is this idea of sex.

The entire cathedral symbolized the crucified body of Christ; its two towers, man and woman—that Adam and Eve, for whose redemption, according to popular belief, Christ suffered and was crucified. The north, or right hand tower ("the man's side") was called the sacred male pillar, Jachin; and the south, or left hand tower ("the woman's side") the sacred female pillar, Boaz, from the two columns flanking the gate to Solomon's Temple —itself an allegory of the bodily temple. In only a few of the French cathedrals is this distinction clearly and consistently maintained, and of these Tours forms perhaps the most remarkable example, for in its flamboyant façade, over and above the difference in actual breadth and apparent sturdiness of the two towers (the south being the more slender and delicate), there is a clearly marked distinction in the character of the ornamentation, that of the north tower being more salient, angular, radial—more masculine, in point of fact (Illustration 17). In Notre Dame, the cathedral of Paris, as in the cathedral of Tours, the north tower is perceptibly broader than the south. The only

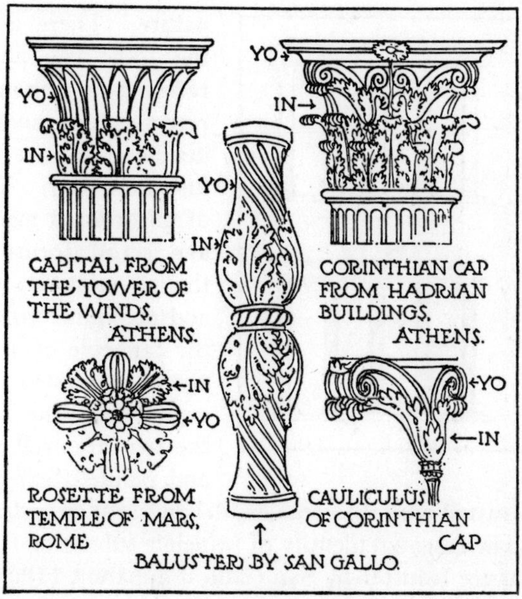

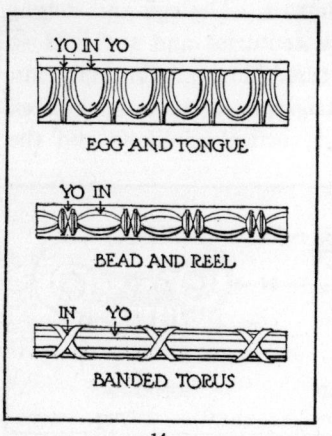

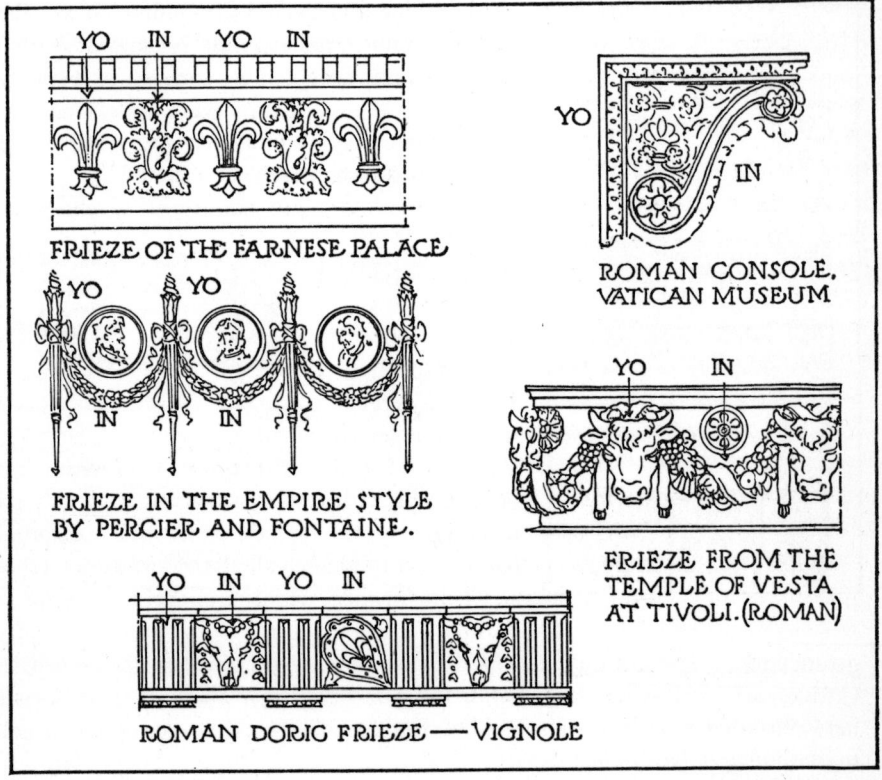

15

other important difference appears to be in the angular label mould above the north entrance: whatever may have been its original function or significance, it serves to define the tower sexually, so to speak, as effectively as does the beard on a man's face. In Amiens the north tower is taller than the south, and more massive in its upper stages. The only traceable indication of sex in the ornamentation occurs in the spandrels at the sides of the entrance arches: those of the north tower containing single circles, and those of the south tower containing two. This difference, small as it may seem, is significant, for in Europe during the Middle Ages, just as anciently in Egypt, and again in Greece—in fact wherever and whenever the Secret Doctrine was known—sex was attributed to numbers, odd numbers being conceived of

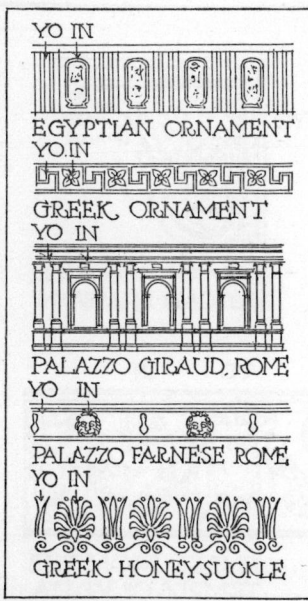

16

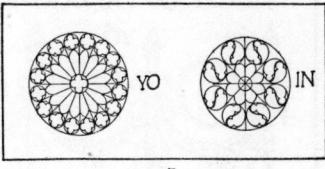

17

as masculine and even as feminine. Two, the first feminine number, thus became a symbol of femininity, accepted as such so universally at the time the cathedrals were built, that two strokes of a bell announced the death of a woman, three the death of a man.

The vital, organic quality so conspicuous in the best Gothic architecture has been attributed to the fact that necessity determined its characteristic forms. Professor Goodyear has demonstrated that it may be due also in part to certain subtle vertical leans and horizontal bends; and to nicely calculated variations from strict uniformity, which find their analogue in nature, where structure is seldom rigidly geometrical. The author hazards the theory that still another reason why a Gothic cathedral seems so living a thing is because it abounds in contrasts between what, for lack of more descriptive adjectives, he is forced to call masculine and feminine forms.

Ruskin says, in "Stones of Venice," "All good Gothic is nothing more than the development, in various ways, and on every conceivable scale, of the group formed by the pointed arch for the bearing line below, and the gable for the protecting line above, and from the huge, gray, shaly slope of the cathedral roof, with its elastic pointed vaults beneath, to the crown-like points that enrich the smallest niche of its doorway, one law and one expression will be found in all. The modes of support and of decoration are infinitely various, but the real character of the building, in all good Gothic, depends on the single lines of the gable over the pointed arch

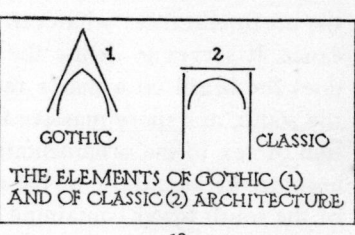

18

endlessly rearranged and repeated." These two, an angular and a curved form, like the everywhere recurring column and lintel of classic architecture, are but presentments of Yo and In (Illustration 18). Every Gothic traceried window, with straight and vertical mullions in the rectangle, losing themselves in the intricate foliations of the arch, celebrates the marriage of this ever diverse pair. The circle and the triangle are the In and Yo of Gothic tracery, its Eve and Adam, as it were, for from their union springs that progeny of trefoil, quatrefoil, cinquefoil, of shapes flowing like water, and shapes darting like flame, which make such visible music to the entranced eye.

By seeking to discover In and Yo in their myriad manifestations, by learning to discriminate between them, and by attempting to express their characteristic qualities in new forms of beauty—from the disposition of a façade to the shaping of a moulding—the architectural designer will charge his work with that esoteric significance, that excess of beauty, by which architecture rises to the dignity of a "fine" art (Illustrations 19, 20). In so doing, however, he should never forget, and the layman, also, should ever remember, that the supreme architectural excellence is fitness, appropriateness, the perfect adaptation of means to ends, and the perfect expression of both means and ends. These two aims, the one abstract and universal, the other concrete and individual, can always be combined, just as in every human countenance are combined a type, which is universal, and a character, which is individual.

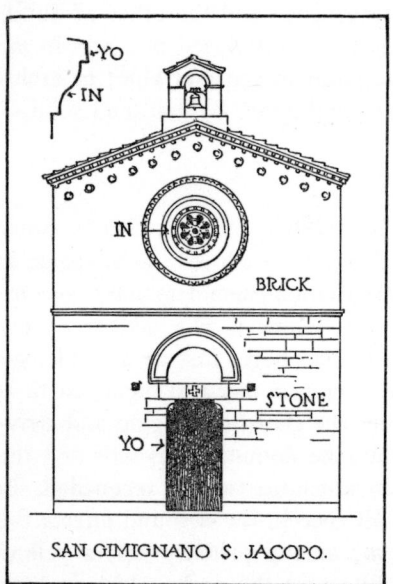

III

CHANGELESS CHANGE

TRINITY, CONSONANCE, DIVERSITY IN MONOTONY,
BALANCE, RHYTHMIC CHANGE, RADIATION

THE preceding essay was devoted for the most part to that "inevitable duality" which finds concrete expression in countless pairs of opposites, such as day and night, fire and water, man and woman; in the art of music by two chords, one of suspense and the other of fulfilment; in speech by vowel and consonant sounds, epitomized in *a* and in *m;* in painting by warm colors and cold, epitomized in red and blue; in architecture by the vertical column and the horizontal lintel, by void and solid,— and so on.

TRINITY

This concept should now be modified by another, namely: that in every duality a third is latent; that two implies three, for each sex, so to speak, is in process of becoming the other, and this alternation engenders and is accomplished by means of a third term, or neuter, which is like neither of the original two, but partakes of the nature of them both, just as a child may resembles both its parents. Twilight comes between day and night; earth is the child of fire and water; in music, besides the chord of longing and striving and the chord of rest and satisfaction (the dominant seventh and the tonic) there is a third, or resolving chord, in which the two are reconciled. In the sacred syllable Om, which epitomizes all speech, the *u* sound effects the transition between the *a* sound and the *m;* among primary colors yellow comes between red and blue; and in architecture the arch, which is both weight and support, which is neither vertical nor horizontal, may be considered the neuter of the group of which the column and the lintel are respectively masculine and feminine. "These are the three," says Mr. Louis Sullivan, "the only three letters from which has been expanded the architectural art, as a great and superb language wherewith man has expressed, through the generations, the changing drift of his thoughts."

It would be supererogatory to dwell at any length on this "trinity of manifestation" as the concrete expression of that unmanifest and mystical trinity, that *three-in-one* which under various names occurs in every world-religion, where, defying definition, it was wont to find expression symbolically, in some combination of vertical, horizontal, and curved lines. The ansated cross of the Egyptians is such a symbol, the Buddhist wheel, and the flyflot, or swastika inscribed within a circle; also those numerous Christian symbols combining the circle and the cross. Such ideographs have spelled profound meaning to the thinkers of past ages. We of to-day are not given to discovering anything wonderful in three strokes of a pen, but every artist, in the weaving of his pattern, must needs employ these mystic symbols, in one form or another, and if he employs them with a full sense of their hidden meaning, his work will be apt to gain in originality and beauty,—for originality is a new and personal perception of beauty, and beauty is the name we give to truth we cannot understand.

In architecture, this trinity of vertical, horizontal and curved lines finds admirable illustration in the application of columns and entablature to an arch and impost construction, so common in Roman and Renaissance work. This is a redundancy, and finds no justification in the reason, since the weight is sustained by the arch, and the "order" is an appendage merely, yet the combination, illogical as it is, satisfies the sense of beauty, because the arch effects a transition between the columns and the entablature, and completes the trinity of vertical, horizontal, and curved lines (Illustration 21). In the entrances to many of the Gothic cathedrals and churches the same elements are better because more logically disposed. Here the horizontal lintel and its vertical supports are not decorative merely, but really perform their proper functions, while the arch, too, has a raison d'etre in that it serves to relieve the lintel of the superincumbent weight of masonry. The same arrangement sometimes occurs in Classic architecture also, as when an opening spanned by a single arch is subdivided by means of an order (Illustration 22).

Three is pre-eminently the number of architecture, because it is the number of our space, which is three-dimensional, and of all the arts architecture is most concerned with the expression of spatial relations. The division of a composition into three related parts is so universal that it would seem to be the result of an instinctive action of the human mind. The twin pylons of an Egyptian temple, with its entrance between, for a third division, has its correspondence in the two towers of a Gothic cathedral and the intervening screen wall of the nave. In the palaces of the Renaissance a three-fold division—vertically by means of quoins or pilasters, and horizontally by means of cornices or string courses—was common, as was also the division into a principal and two subordinate masses (Illustration 23).

The architectural "orders," so-called, are divided threefold into pedestal or stylobate, column, and entablature; and each of these is again divided threefold; the first into plinth, die, and cornice; the second into base, shaft, and capital; the third into architrave, frieze, and cornice. In many cases these again lend themselves to a threefold subdivision. A more detailed analysis of the capitals already shown to be twofold reveals a third member:

THE LAW OF TRINITY: A THREEFOLD DISPOSITION OF THE PARTS OF A BUILDING

- GREEK — THE ERECTHEUM.
- ITALIAN RENAISSANCE PALAZZO VENDRAMIN-CALERGI AT VENICE.
- PALAZZO BARIOLINI, FLORENCE.
- GOTHIC — NOTRE DAME.
- EGYPTIAN — FRONT OF TEMPLE.
- FRENCH RENAISSANCE — CHATEAU DE BEAUMESNIL.

23

in the Greek Doric this consists of the annulets immediately below the abacus; in the other orders, the necking which divides the shaft from the cap.

CONSONANCE

"As is the small, so is the great" is a perpetually recurring phrase in the literature of theosophy, and naturally so, for it is a succint statement of a fundamental and far-reaching truth. The scientist recognizes it now and then, and here and there, but the occultist trusts it always and utterly. To him the microcosm and the macrocosm are one and the same in essence, and the forth-going impulse which calls a universe into being and the indrawing impulse which extinguishes it again, each lasting millions of years, are echoed and repeated in the inflow and outflow of the breath through the nostrils, in nutrition and excretion, in daily activity and nightly rest, in that longer day which we name a lifetime, and that longer rest in Devachan, and so on, up and up and up, and forever and ever and ever.

In the same way, in nature, a thing is echoed and repeated throughout its parts. Each leaf on a tree is itself a tree in miniature, each blossom a modified leaf; every vertebrate animal is a complicated system of spines; the ripple is the wave of a larger wave, and that larger wave is part of the ebbing and flowing tide. In music this law is illustrated in the return of the tonic

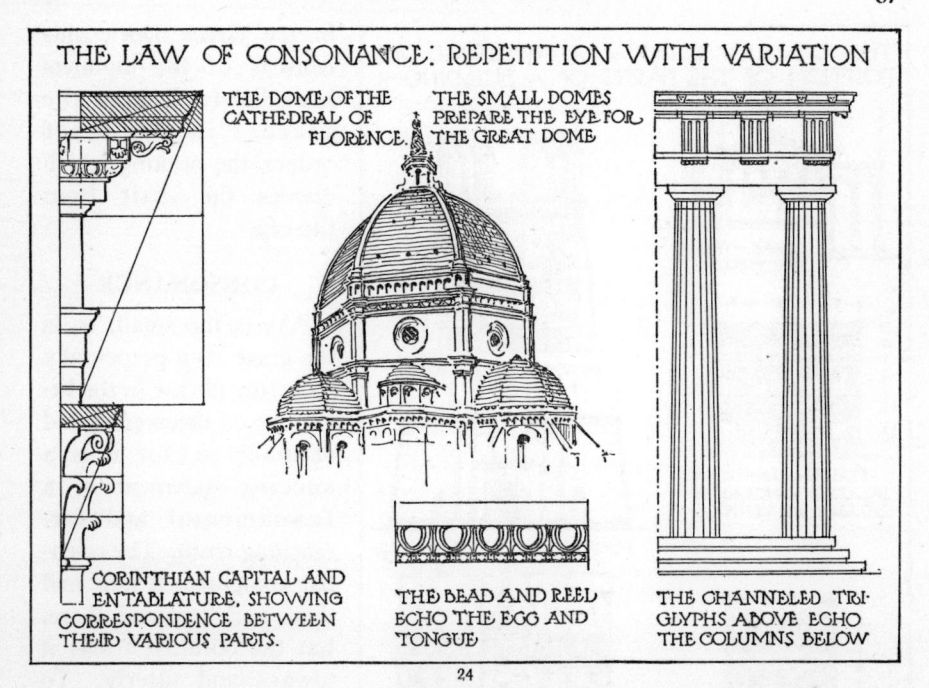

THE LAW OF CONSONANCE: REPETITION WITH VARIATION

CORINTHIAN CAPITAL AND ENTABLATURE, SHOWING CORRESPONDENCE BETWEEN THEIR VARIOUS PARTS.

THE DOME OF THE CATHEDRAL OF FLORENCE. THE SMALL DOMES PREPARE THE EYE FOR THE GREAT DOME

THE BEAD AND REEL ECHO THE EGG AND TONGUE

THE CHANNELED TRIGLYPHS ABOVE ECHO THE COLUMNS BELOW

24

to itself in the octave, and its partial return in the dominant; also, in a more extended sense, in the repetition of a major theme in the minor, or in the treble and again in the bass, with modifications, perhaps, of time and key. In the art of painting the law is exemplified in the repetition with variation of certain colors and combinations of lines in different parts of the same picture, so disposed as to lead the eye to some focal point. Every painter knows that any important color in his picture must be echoed, as it were, in different places, for harmony of the whole.

In the drama the repetition of a speech, or of an entire scene, but under circumstances which give it a different meaning, is often very effective, as when Gratiano, in the trial scene of The Merchant of Venice taunts Shylock with his own words, "A Daniel come to judgment!" or, as when, in one of the later scenes of As You Like It, an earlier scene is repeated, but with Rosalind speaking in her proper person and no longer as the boy Ganymede.

These recurrences, these inner consonances, these repetitions with variations are common in architecture also. The channeled triglyphs of a Greek

THE LAW OF CONSONANCE

ONE BAY OF THE "ANGEL CHOIRS" OF LINCOLN CATHEDRAL

THE SAME MOTIF REPEATED WITH VARIATIONS

25

Doric frieze echo the fluted columns below (Illustration 24). The balustrade which crowns a colonnade is a repetition, in some sort, of the colonnade itself. The modillions of a Corinthian cornice are but elaborate and embellished dentils. Each pinnacle of a Gothic cathedral is a little tower with its spire. As Ruskin has pointed out, the great vault of the cathedral nave, together with the pointed roof above it, is repeated in the entrance arch with its gable, and the same two elements appear in every statue-enshrining niche of the doorway. In Classic architecture, as has been shown, instead of the pointed arch and gable, the column and entablature everywhere recur under different

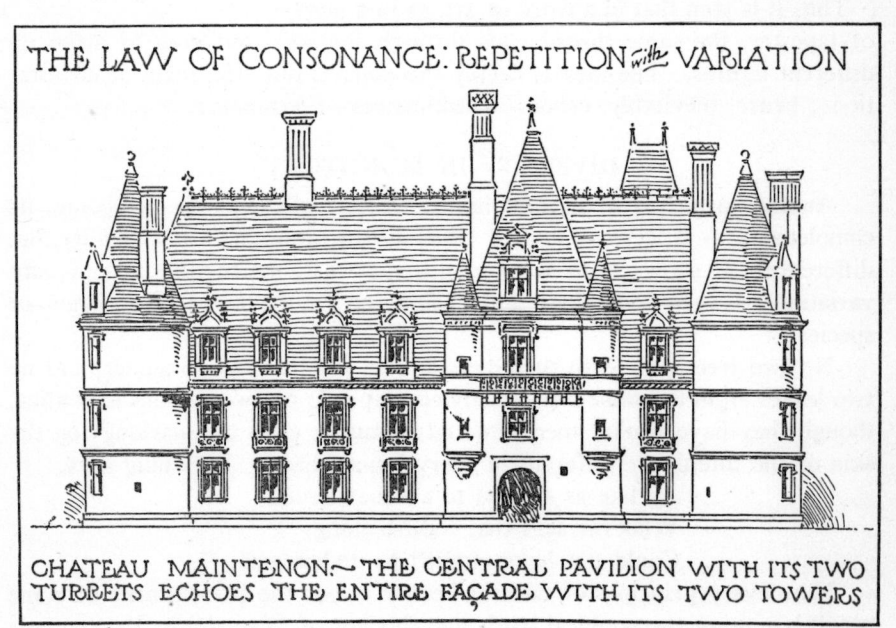

THE LAW OF CONSONANCE: REPETITION with VARIATION

CHATEAU MAINTENON.— THE CENTRAL PAVILION WITH ITS TWO TURRETS ECHOES THE ENTIRE FAÇADE WITH ITS TWO TOWERS

26

forms. The minor domes which flank the great dome of the cathedral of Florence enhance and reinforce the latter, and prepare the eye for a climax which would otherwise be too abrupt. The central pavilion of the Chateau Maintenon, with its two turrets, echoes the entire façade with its two towers. Like the overture to an opera, it introduces themes which find a more extended development elsewhere (Illustration 26).

This law of Consonance is operative in architecture more obscurely in the form of recurring numerical ratios, identical geometrical determining figures, parallel diagonals, and the like, which will be discussed in a subsequent essay. It has also to do with style and scale, the adherence to substantially one method of construction and manner of ornament, just as in music the key, or chosen series of notes may not be departed from except through proper modulations, or in a specific manner.

Thus it is seen that in a work of art, as in a piece of tapestry, the same thread runs through the web, but goes to make up different figures. The idea is deeply theosophic: one life, many manifestations; hence, inevitably, echoes, resemblances—*Consonance.*

DIVERSITY IN MONOTONY

Another principle of natural beauty, closely allied to the foregoing, its complement, as it were, is that of Diversity in Monotony—not identity, but difference. It shows itself for the most part as a perceptible and piquant variation between individual units belonging to the same class, type, or species.

No two trees put forth their branches in just the same manner, and no two leaves from the same tree exactly correspond; no two persons look alike, though they have similar members and features; even the markings on the skin of the thumb are different in every human hand. Browning says,

"As like as a hand to another hand!
Whoever said that foolish thing,
Could not have studied to understand—"

Now every principle of natural beauty is but the presentment of some occult law, some theosophical truth, and this law of Diversity in Monotony is

40　　　THE BEAUTIFUL NECESSITY　　　III

THE LAW OF DIVERSITY IN MONOTONY

THREE PANELS OF BASE "A"

DETAILS FROM THE TEMPLE OF APOLLO NEAR MILETUS

28

the presentment of the truth that identity does not exclude individuality. The law is binding, yet the will is free: all men are brothers, bound by the ties of brotherhood, yet each is unique, a free agent, and never so free as

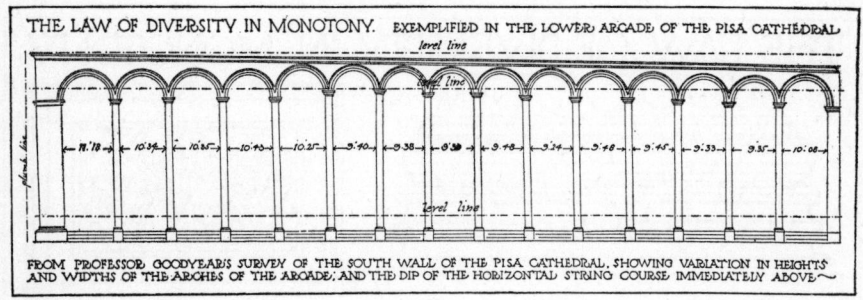

THE LAW OF DIVERSITY IN MONOTONY. EXEMPLIFIED IN THE LOWER ARCADE OF THE PISA CATHEDRAL

FROM PROFESSOR GOODYEAR'S SURVEY OF THE SOUTH WALL OF THE PISA CATHEDRAL, SHOWING VARIATION IN HEIGHTS AND WIDTHS OF THE ARCHES OF THE ARCADE; AND THE DIP OF THE HORIZONTAL STRING COURSE IMMEDIATELY ABOVE

29

when most bound by the Good Law. This truth nature beautifully proclaims, and art also. In architecture it is admirably exemplified in the metopes of the Parthenon frieze: seen at a distance these must have presented a scarcely distinguishable texture of sunlit marble and cool shadow, yet in reality, each is a separate work of art. So with the capitals of the columns of the wonderful sea-arcade of the Venetian Ducal palace: alike in general contour they differ widely in detail, and unfold a Bible story. In Gothic cathedrals, in Romanesque monastery cloisters, a teeming variety of invention is hidden beneath apparent uniformity. The gargoyles of Notre Dame make similar silhouettes against the sky, but seen near at hand, what a menagerie of monsters! The same spirit of controlled individuality, of liberty subservient to the law of all, is exemplified in the bases of the columns of the temple of Apollo near Mitelus,—each one a separate masterpiece of various ornamentation adorning an established architectural form (Illustration 28).

The builders of the early Italian churches, instinctively obeying this law of Diversity in Monotony, varied the size of the arches in the same arcade (Illustration 29), and that this was an effect of art and not of accident or carelessness Ruskin long ago discovered, and the Brooklyn Institute surveys have amply confirmed his view. Although by these means the builders of that day produced effects of deceptive perspective, of subtle concord and contrast, their sheer hatred of monotony and meaningless repetition may have led them to diversify their arcades in the manner described, for a rigidly equal and regular division lacks interest and vitality.

BALANCE

If one were to establish an axial plane vertically through the center of a tree, in most cases it would be found that the masses of foliage, however irregularly shaped on either side of such an axis, just about balanced one another. Similarly, in all our bodily movements, for every change of equilibrium there occurs an opposition and adjustment of members of such a nature that an axial plane through the center of gravity would divide the body into two substantially equal masses, as in the case of the tree. This physical plane law of Balance, shows itself for the most part on the higher planes, as the law of Compensation, whereby, to the vision of the occultist, all accounts are "squared," so to speak. It is, in effect, the law of Justice, aptly symbolized by the scales.

The law of Balance finds abundant illustration in art: in music by the opposition, the answering, of one phrase by another of the same length and elements, but involving a different succession of intervals; in painting by the disposition of masses in such a way that they about equalize one another, so that there is no sense of "strain" in the composition.

In architecture the common and obvious recognition of the law of Balance is in the symmetrical disposition of the elements, whether of plan or of elevation, on either side of axial lines. A far more subtle and vital exhibition of the law occurs when the opposed elements do not exactly match, but differ from one another, as in the case of the two towers of Amiens, for example. This sort of balance may be said to be characteristic of Gothic, as symmetry is characteristic of Classic architecture.

RHYTHMIC CHANGE

There is in nature a universal tendency towards refinement and compactness of form in space, or contrariwise, towards increment and diffusion; and this manifests itself in time as acceleration or retardation. It is governed, in either case, by an exact mathematical law, like the law of falling bodies. It shows itself in the widening circles which appear when one drops a stone in still water, in the convolutions of shells, in the branching of trees, and the veining of leaves; the diminution in the size of the pipes of an organ illustrates it, and the spacing of the frets of a guitar. More and more science is coming to recognize, what theosophy has ever affirmed, that the spiral vortex, which so beautifully illustrates this law, both in its time and its space aspects, is the universal archetype, the pattern of all that is, has been, or will be, since it is the shape assumed by the ultimate physical atom, and the ultimate physical atom is the physical cosmos in miniature.

This Rhythmic Diminution is everywhere: it is in the eye itself, for any series of mathematically equal units, such, for example, as the columns and intercolumnations of a colonnade, become, when seen in perspective, rhythmically unequal, diminishing according to the universal law. The entasis of a Classic column is determined by this law, the spirals of the Ionic volute, the annulets of the Parthenon cap, obey it (Illustration 30).

In recognition of the same principle of Rhythmic Diminution a building is often made to grow, or to appear to grow lighter, more intricate, finer, from the ground upwards; an end attained by various devices, one of the most common being the employment of the more attenuated and highly ornamented orders above the simpler and sturdier, as in the Roman Colosseum, or in the Palazzo Uguccioni, in Florence, to mention only two examples out of a great number. In the Riccardi Palace an effect of increasing refinement is obtained by diminishing the boldness of the rustication of the ashlar in successive stories; in the Farnese, by the gradual reduction of the size of the angle quoins (Illustration 30). In an Egyptian pylon it is achieved most simply by battering the wall; in a Gothic cathedral most elaborately, by a kind of segregation, or breaking up, analogous to that which a tree undergoes,—the strong, relatively unbroken base corresponding to the trunk, the diminishing buttresses to the tapering limbs, and the multitude of delicate pinnacles and crockets, to the outermost branches and twigs, seen against the sky.

RADIATION

The final principle of natural beauty to which the author would call attention is the law of Radiation, which is, in a manner, a return to the first, the law of Unity. The various parts of any organism radiate from, or otherwise refer back to common centers, or foci, and these to centers of their own. The law is represented in its simplicity in the star fish, in its complexity in the body of man; a tree springs from a seed, the solar system centers in the sun.

The idea here expressed by the term *radiation* is a familiar one to all students of theosophy. The Logos radiates his life and light throughout his universe, bringing into activity a host of entities which become themselves radial centers; these generate still others, and so on endlessly. This principle, like every other, patiently publishes itself to us, unheeding, everywhere in nature, and in all great art as well; it is a law of optics, for example,

44 THE BEAUTIFUL NECESSITY III

THE LAW OF RHYTHMIC DIMINUTION

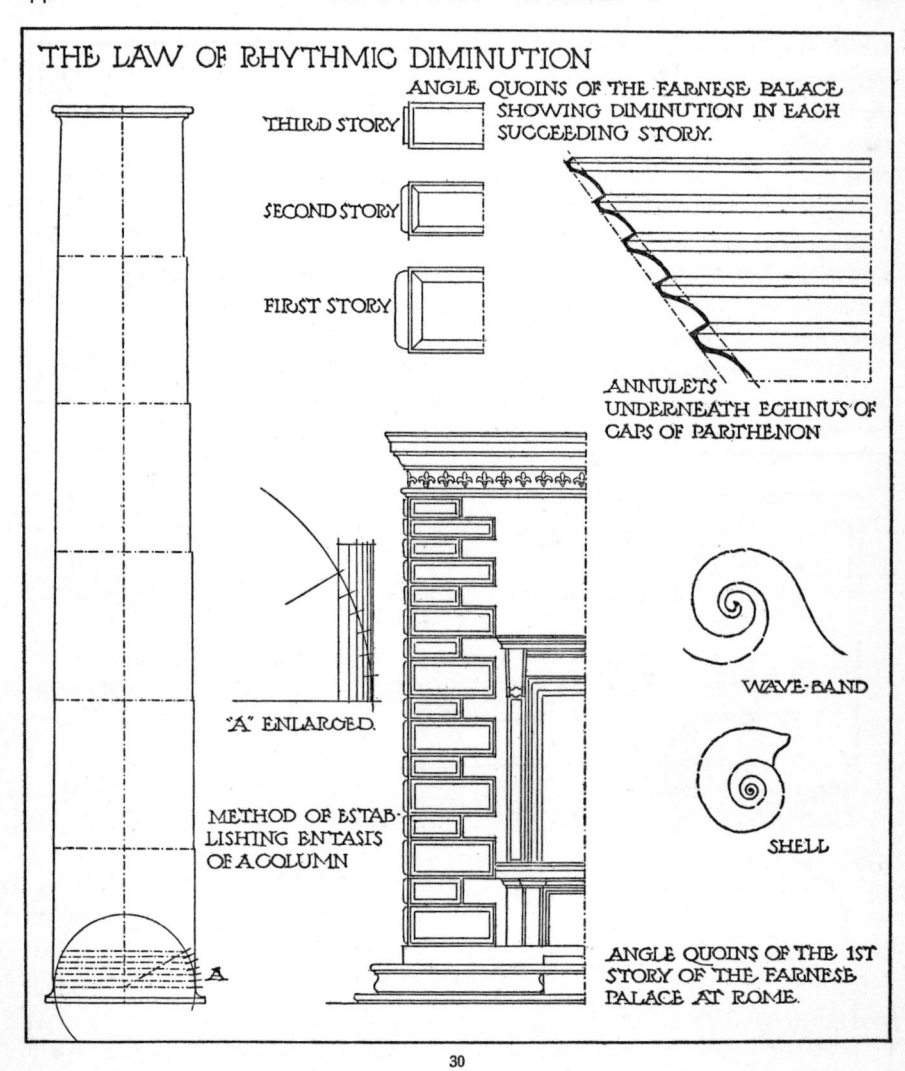

ANGLE QUOINS OF THE FARNESE PALACE, SHOWING DIMINUTION IN EACH SUCCEEDING STORY.

THIRD STORY

SECOND STORY

FIRST STORY

ANNULETS UNDERNEATH ECHINUS OF CAPS OF PARTHENON

"A" ENLARGED.

METHOD OF ESTABLISHING ENTASIS OF A COLUMN

WAVE-BAND

SHELL

ANGLE QUOINS OF THE 1ST STORY OF THE FARNESE PALACE AT ROME.

30

that all straight lines having a common direction if sufficiently prolonged appear to meet in a point, i. e., radiate from it (Illustration 31). Leonardo da Vinci employed this principle of perspective in his Last Supper to draw the spectator's eye to the picture's central figure, the point of sight towards

CHANGELESS CHANGE

which the lines of the walls and ceiling converge centering in the head of Christ. Puvis de Chavannes, in his Boston Library decoration, leads the eye, by a system of triangulation, to the small figure of the Genius of Enlightenment above the central door (Illustration 32); and Ruskin, in his Elements of Drawing, has shown how artfully Turner arranged some of his composition to attract attention to a focal point.

This law of Radiation enters largely into architecture. The Colosseum, based upon the

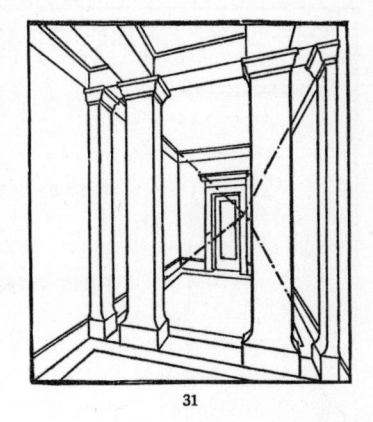

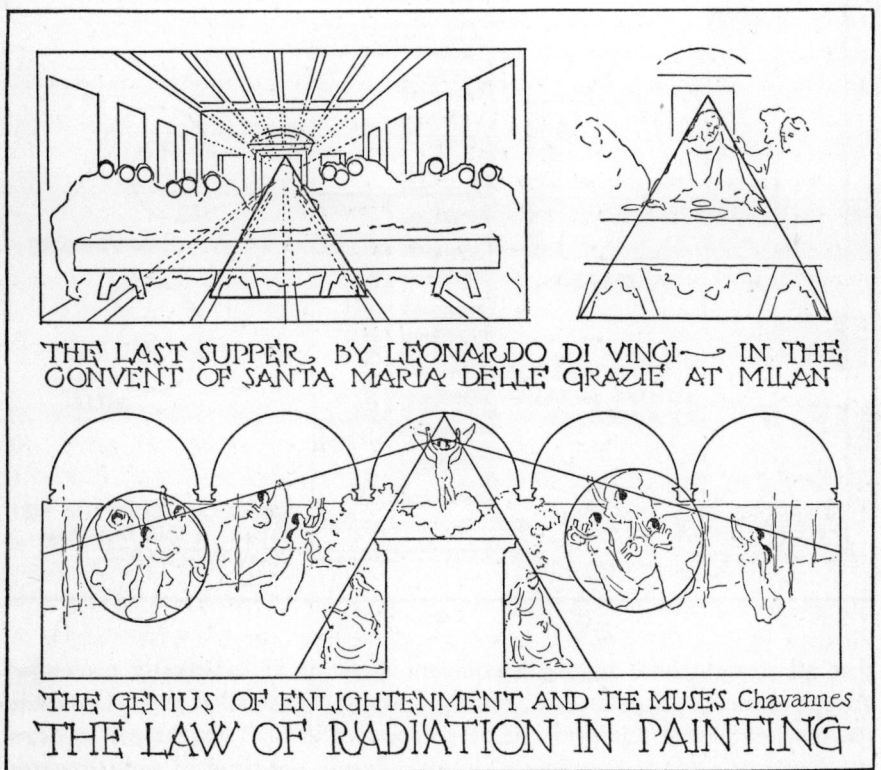

31

THE LAST SUPPER BY LEONARDO DI VINCI — IN THE CONVENT OF SANTA MARIA DELLE GRAZIE AT MILAN

THE GENIUS OF ENLIGHTENMENT AND THE MUSES Chavannes
THE LAW OF RADIATION IN PAINTING

32

ellipse, a figure generated from two points, or foci, and the Pantheon, based upon the circle, a figure generated from a single center, are familiar examples. The distinctive characteristic of Gothic construction, the concentration or focalization of the weight of the vaults and arches at certain points, is another illustration of the same principle applied to architecture, beautifully exemplified in the semi-circular apse of a cathedral, where the lines of the plan converge to a common center, and the ribs of the vaulting meet upon the capitals of the piers and columns, seeming to radiate thence to still other centers in the loftier vaults which finally meet in a center common to all.

The tracery of the great roses high up in the façades of the cathedrals of Paris and of Amiens illustrate Radiation,—in the one case masculine: straight, angular, direct; in the other feminine: curved, flowing, sinuous.

The same Beautiful Necessity determined the characteristics of much of the ornament of widely separated styles and periods: the Egyptian lotus, the Greek honeysuckle, the Roman acanthus, Gothic leaf work—to snatch at random four blossoms from the sheaf of time. The radial principle still inherent in the debased ornament of the late Renaissance gives that ornament a unity, a coherence, and a kind of beauty all its own (Illustration 35).

Such are a few of the more obvious laws of natural beauty and their application to the art of architecture. The list is by no means exhausted, but it is not the multiplicity and diversity of laws which it is important to keep in mind, so much as their essential unity and co-ordination, for they are but different aspects of the One Law, that whereby the Logos manifests himself in time and space. A brief recapitulation will serve to make this correlation plain, and at the same time fix what has been written more firmly in the reader's mind.

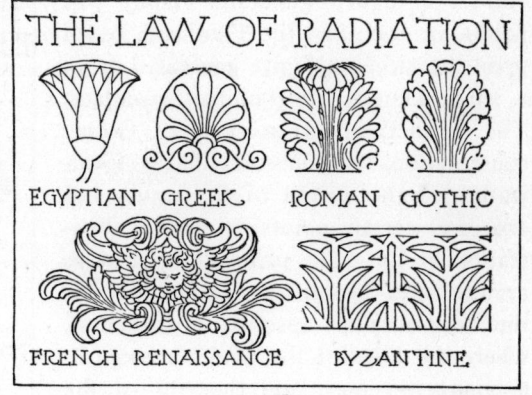

First comes the law of *Unity;* then, since every unit is, in its essence, twofold, there is the law of *Polarity;* but this duality is not static, but dynamic, the two parts acting and reacting upon one another to produce a third, hence the law of *Trinity.* Given this third term, and the innumerable combinations made possible by its relations to and reaction upon the original pair, the law of *Multiplicity in Unity* naturally follows, as does the law of *Consonance,* or repetition, since the primal process of differentiation tends to repeat itself, and the original combination to reappear,—but to reappear in changed form, hence the law of *Diversity in Monotony.* The law of *Balance* is seen to be but a modification of the law of Polarity, and since all things are waxing and waning, there is the law whereby they wax and wane, that of *Rhythmic Change. Radiation* rediscovers and reaffirms, even in the utmost complexity, that essential and fundamental unity from which complexity was wrought.

Everything, beautiful or ugly, obeys and illustrates one or another of these laws, so universal are they, so inseparably attendant upon every kind of manifestation in time and space. It is the number of them which finds illustration within small compass, as it were, and the aptness and completeness of such illustration which makes for beauty, because beauty is the fine flower of a sort of sublime ingenuity. A work of art is nothing if not artful: like an acrostic, the more different ways it can be read—up, down, across, from right to left and from left to right—the better it is, other things being equal. This statement, of course, may be construed in such a way as to appear absurd; what is meant is simply that the more a work of art is freighted and fraught with meaning beyond meaning, the more secure its immortality, the more powerful its appeal. For enjoyment, it is not necessary that all these meanings should be fathomed, it is only necessary that they should be felt.

Consider for a moment the manner in which Leonardo da Vinci's Last Supper, an acknowledged masterpiece, conforms to every one of the laws of beauty enumerated above (Illustration 32). It illustrates the law of Unity in that it movingly portrays a single significant episode in the life of Christ. The eye is led to dwell upon the central personage of this drama by many artful expedients: the visible part of the figure of Christ conforms to the lines of an equilateral triangle placed exactly in the center of the picture, the figure is separated by a considerable space from the groups of the disciples on either hand, and stands relieved against the largest parallelogram of light, and the vanishing point of the perspective is in the head of Christ, at the apex, therefore, of the triangle. The law of Polarity finds fulfillment in the complex and flowing lines of the draped figures contrasted with the simple parallelogram of the cloth-covered table, and the severe architecture of the room; the law of Trinity is exemplified in the three windows, and in the subdivision of the twelve figures of the disciples into four groups of three figures each. The law of Consonance appears in the repetition of the horizontal lines of the table in the ceiling above; and in the central triangle before referred to, continued and echoed, as it were, in the triangular supports of the table visible underneath the cloth. The law of Diversity in Monotony is illustrated in the varying disposition of the heads of the figures in the four groups of three; the law of Balance in the essential symmetry of the entire composition; the law of Rhythmic Change in the diminishing of the wall and ceiling spaces, and the law of Radiation in the convergence of all the perspective lines to a single significant point.

To illustrate further the universality of these laws, consider now their application to a single work of architecture: the Taj Mahal, one of the most beautiful buildings of the world (Illustration 36). It is a unit, but twofold, for it consists of a curved part and an angular part, roughly figured as an inverted cup upon a cube; each of these (seen in parallel perspective, at the end of the principal vista) is threefold, for there are two sides and a central parallelogram, and two lesser domes flank the great dome. The composition is rich in consonances, for the side arches echo the central one, the subordinate domes, the great dome, and the lanterns of the outstanding minarets repeat the principal motif. Diversity in Monotony appears abundantly in the ornament, which is intricate and infinitely various; the law of Balance is everywhere operative in the symmetry of the entire design. Rhythmic Change appears in the tapering of the minarets, the outlines of the domes and their mass relations to one another; and finally, the whole effect is of radiation from a central point, of elements disposed on radial lines.

It would be fatuous to contend that the prime object of a work of architecture is to obey and illustrate these laws. The prime object of a work of architecture is to fulfill certain definite conditions in a practical, economical, and admirable way, and in fulfilling to express as far as possible these conditions and the manner of their fulfilment. The architect who is also an artist, however, will do this and something beyond. Working for the most part unconsciously, harmoniously, joyfully, his building will obey and illustrate natural laws—these laws of beauty—and to the extent it does so, it will be a work of art, for art is the method of nature carried into those higher regions of thought and feeling which man alone inhabits: regions which it is one of the missions of theosophy to explore.

IV

THE BODILY TEMPLE

CARLYLE says: "There is but one temple in the world, and that is the body of man." If the body is, as he declares, a temple, it is not less true that a temple or any work of architectural art is a larger body which man has created for his uses, just as the individual self is housed within its stronghold of flesh and bones. Architectural beauty, like human beauty, depends upon the proper subordination of parts to the whole, the harmonious interrelation between these parts, the expressiveness of each of its function or functions, and when these are many and diverse, their reconcilement one with another. This being so, a study of the human figure with a view to analyzing the sources of its beauty cannot fail to be profitable. Pursued intelligently, such a study will stimulate the mind to a perception of those simple yet subtle laws according to which nature everywhere works, and it will educate the eye in the finest known school of proportion, training it to distinguish minute differences, in the same way that the hearing of good music cultivates the ear.

Those principles of natural beauty which formed the subject of the two preceding essays are all exemplified in the ideally perfect human figure. Though essentially a unit, there is a well marked division into right and left. "Hands to hands, and feet to feet, in one body grooms and brides." There are two arms, two legs, two ears, two eyes, and two lids to each eye: the nose has two nostrils, the mouth has two lips. Moreover, the terms of such pairs are masculine and feminine with regard to each other, one being active and the other passive. Owing to the great size and one-sided position of the liver, the right half of the body is heavier than the left; the right arm is usually longer and more muscular than the left; the right eye is slightly higher than its fellow. In speaking and eating the lower jaw and under lip are active and mobile with relation to the upper; in winking it is the upper eyelid which is the more active. That "inevitable duality" which is exhibited in the form of the body characterizes its motions also. In the act of walking for example, a forward movement is attained by means of a forward and a backward movement of the thighs on the axis of the hips; this leg movement becomes twofold again below the knee, and the feet move up and down independently on the axis of the ankle. A similar progression is followed in raising the arm and hand: motion is communicated first to the larger parts, through them to the smaller, and thence to the extremities, becoming more rapid and complex as it progresses, so that all free and natural movements of the limbs describe invisible lines of beauty in the air. Coexistent with this pervasive duality, there is a threefold division of the figure into trunk, head, and limbs, a superior trinity of head and arms, and an inferior trinity of trunk and legs. The limbs are divided threefold into upper-arm, forearm, and hand; thigh, leg, and foot. The hand flowers out into fingers and the foot into toes, each with a threefold articulation; and in this way is effected that transition from unity to multiplicity, from simplicity to complexity, which appears to be so universal throughout nature, and of which a tree is the perfect symbol.

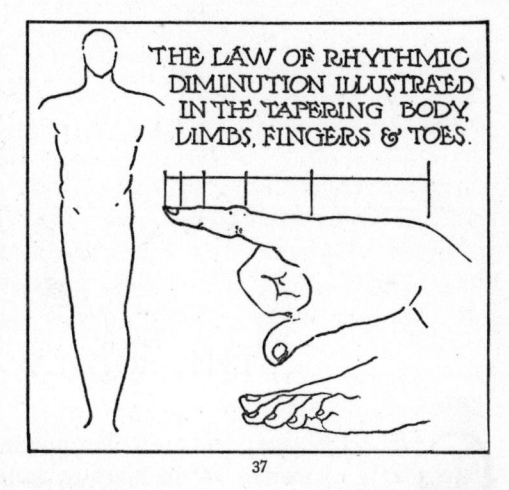

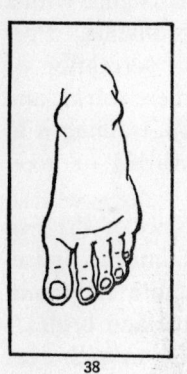

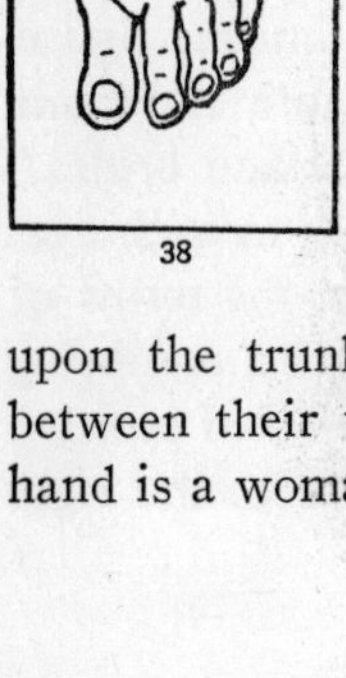

The body is rich in veiled repetitions, echoes, consonances. The head and arms are in a sense a refinement upon the trunk and legs, there being a clearly traceable correspondence between their various parts. The hand is the body in little,—"Your soft hand is a woman of itself,"—the palm, the trunk; the four fingers, the four limbs; and the thumb, the head; each finger is a little arm, each finger tip a little palm. The lips are the lids of the mouth, the lids are the lips of the eyes—and so on. The law of rhythmic diminution is illustrated in the tapering of the entire body and of the limbs, in the graduated sizes and lengths of the fingers and the toes, and in the successively decreasing lengths of the palm and of the joints of the fingers, so that in closing the hand the fingers describe natural spirals (Illustrations 37, 38). Finally, the limbs radiate as it were from the trunk, the fingers from a point in the wrist, the toes from a point in the ankle. The ribs radiate from the spinal column like the veins of a leaf from its midrib (Illustration 39).

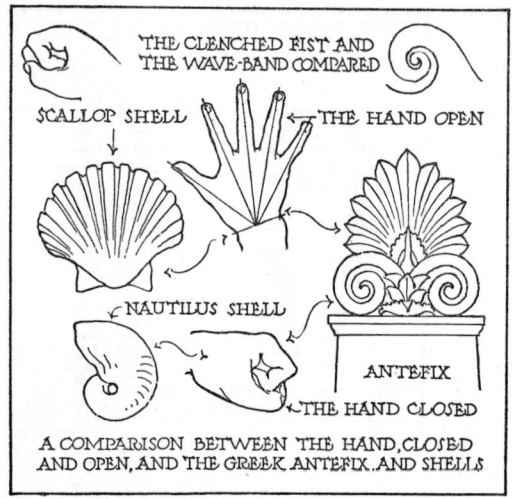

The relation of these laws of beauty to the art of architecture has been shown already. They are reiterated here only to show that man is indeed the microcosm—a little world fashioned from the same elements and in accordance with the same Beautiful Necessity as is the greater world in which he dwells. When he builds a house or temple he builds it not literally in his own image, but according to the laws of his own being, and there are correspondences not altogether fanciful between the animate body of flesh and the inanimate body of stone.

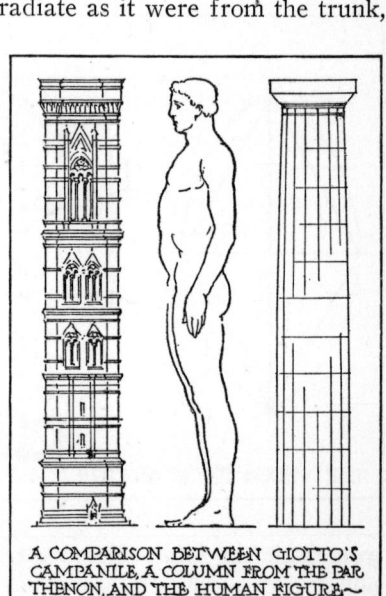

THE BODILY TEMPLE

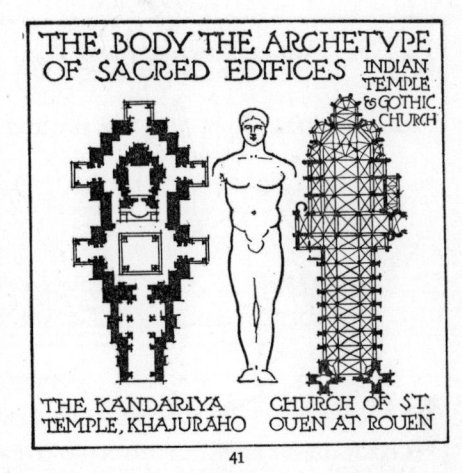

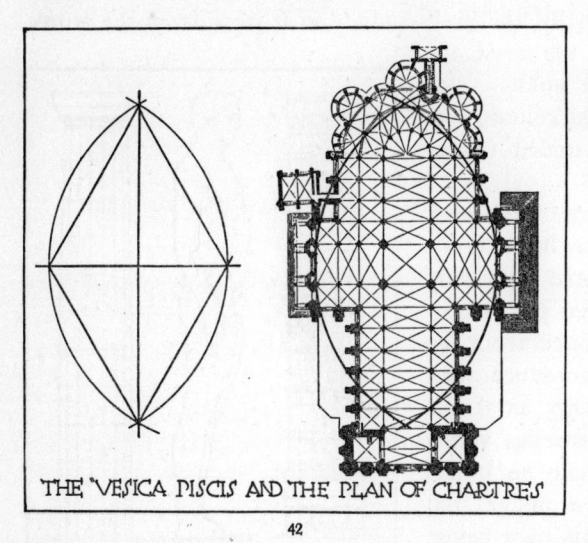

Do we not all of us, consciously or unconsciously, recognize the fact of character and physiognomy in buildings? Are they not, to our imagination, masculine or feminine, winning or forbidding—*human,* in point of fact—to a greater degree that anything else of man's creating? They are this certainly to the true lover and student of architecture. Seen from a distance, the great French cathedrals appear like crouching monsters, half beast, half human: the two towers stand like a man and a woman, mysterious and gigantic, looking out across the city or plain. The campaniles of Italy rise above the churches and houses like the sentinels of a sleeping camp,—nor is their strangely human aspect wholly imaginary: these giants of mountain and campagna have eyes and brazen tongues; rising four square, story above story, with a belfry or lookout, like a head, atop, their likeness to a man is not infrequently enhanced by a certain identity of proportion: of ratio, that is, of height to width— Giotto's beautiful tower is an example. The caryatid is a supporting member in the form of a woman; in the Ionic column we discern her stiffened, like Lot's wife, into a pillar, with nothing to show her feminine but the spirals of her beautiful hair. The columns which uphold the pediment of the Parthenon are as unmistakably masculine: the ratio of their breadth to their height is the ratio of the breadth to the height of a man (Illustration 40).

At certain periods of the world's history, periods of mystical enlightenment, men have been wont to use the human figure, the soul's temple, as a sort of archetype for sacred edifices (Illustration 41). The colossi, with calm, inscrutable faces, which flank the entrance to Egyptian temples; the

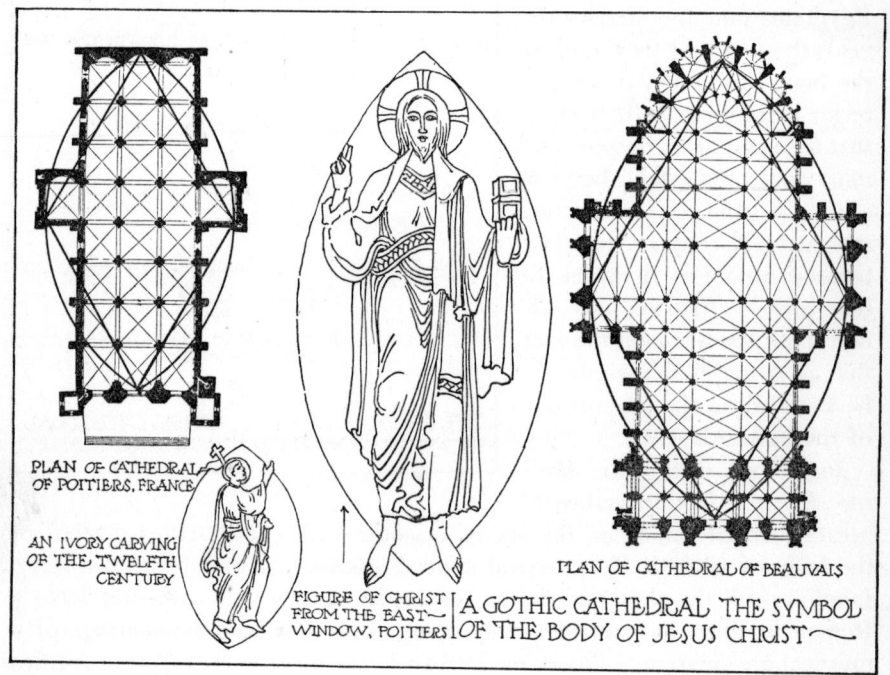

PLAN OF CATHEDRAL OF POITIERS, FRANCE
AN IVORY CARVING OF THE TWELFTH CENTURY
FIGURE OF CHRIST FROM THE EAST WINDOW, POITIERS
A GOTHIC CATHEDRAL THE SYMBOL OF THE BODY OF JESUS CHRIST
PLAN OF CATHEDRAL OF BEAUVAIS

43

great bronze Buddha of Japan, with its dreaming eyes; the little known colossal figures of India—all these belong scarcely less to the domain of architecture than of sculpture. The relation above referred to, however, is a matter more subtle and occult than mere obvious imitation on a large scale, being based upon some correspondence of parts, or similarity of proportions, or both. The correspondence between the innermost sanctuary or shrine of a temple and the heart of a man, and between the gates of that temple and the organs of sense is sufficiently obvious, and a relation once established, the idea is susceptible of almost infinite development. That the ancients proportioned their temples from the human figure is no new idea, nor is it at all surprising. The sculpture of the Egyptians and the Greeks reveals the fact that they studied the body abstractly, in its exterior presentment. It is clear that the rules of its proportions must have been established for sculpture, and it is not unreasonable to suppose that they became canonical in architecture also. Vitruvius and Alberti both lay stress on the fact that all sacred buildings should be founded on the proportions of the human body.

In France, during the Middle Ages, a Gothic cathedral became, at the hands of the secret masonic guilds, a glorified symbol of the body of Christ. To practical-minded students of architectural history, familiar with the slow and halting evolution of a Gothic cathedral from a Roman basilica, such an idea may seem to be only the maunderings of a mystical imagination, a theory evolved from the inner consciousness, entitled to no more consideration than the familiar fallacy that the vaulted nave of a Gothic church was an attempt to imitate the green aisles of a forest. It should be remembered, however, that the habit of the thought of that time was mystical, as that of our own age is utilitarian and scientific; and the chosen language of mysticism is always an elaborate and involved symbolism. What could be more natural than that a building devoted to the worship of a crucified Saviour should be made a symbol, not of the cross only, but of the body crucified?

The *vesica piscis* (a figure formed by the developing arcs of two

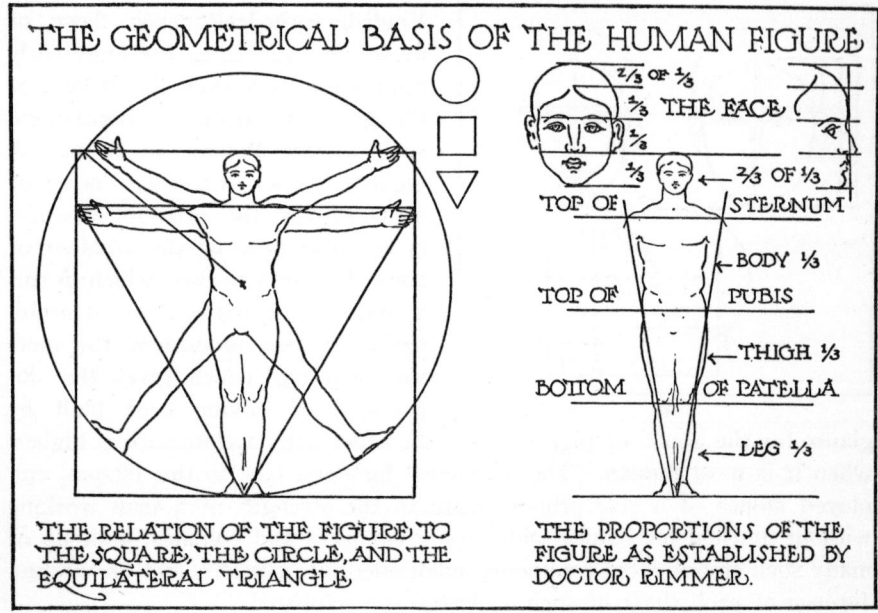

THE GEOMETRICAL BASIS OF THE HUMAN FIGURE

THE RELATION OF THE FIGURE TO THE SQUARE, THE CIRCLE, AND THE EQUILATERAL TRIANGLE.

THE PROPORTIONS OF THE FIGURE AS ESTABLISHED BY DOCTOR RIMMER.

45

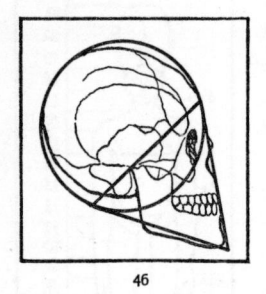

46

equilateral triangles having common side) which in so many cases seems to have determined the main proportion of a cathedral plan—the interior length and the width across the transepts—appears as an aureole around the figure of Christ in early representations, a fact which certainly points to a relation between the two (Illustrations 42, 43). A curious little book, The Rosicrucians, by Hargrave Jennings, contains an interesting diagram which well illustrates this conception of the symbolism of a cathedral. A copy of it is here given. The apse is seen to correspond with the head of Christ, the north transept to his right hand, the south transept to the left hand, the nave to the body, and the north and south towers to the right and left feet respectively (Illustration 44).

The cathedral builders excelled all others in the artfulness with which they established and maintained a relation between their architecture and the stature of a man. This is perhaps one reason why the French and

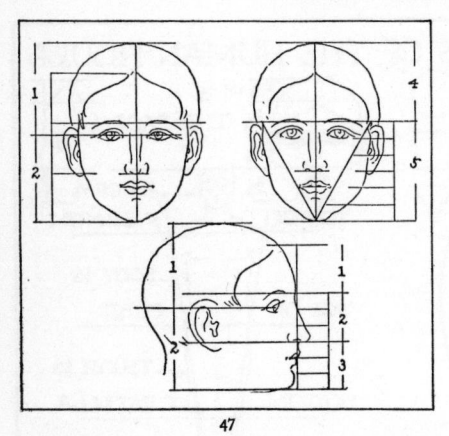

English cathedrals, even those of moderate dimensions, are more truly impressive than even the largest of the great Renaissance structures, such as St. Peter's, in Rome. A gigantic order furnishes no true measure for the eye: its vastness is revealed only by the accident of some human presence which forms a basis of comparison. That architecture is not necessarily the most awe-inspiring which gives the impression of having been built by giants for the abode of pigmies; like the other arts, architecture is highest when it is most human. The mediaeval builders, true to this dictum, employed stones of a size proportionate to the strength of a man working without unusual mechanical aids; the great piers and columns, built up of many such stones, were commonly subdivided into clusters, and the circumference of each shaft of such a cluster approximated the girth of a man; by this device the mouldings of the base and the foliation of the caps were easily kept in scale. Wherever a balustrade occurred it was proportioned, not with relation to the height of the wall or column below, as in classic architecture, but with relation to a man's stature.

It may be stated as a general rule that every work of architecture, of whatever style, should have somewhere about it something fixed and enduring to relate it to the human figure, if it be only a flight of steps in which each one is the measure of a stride. In the Farnese, the Riccardi, the Strozzi, and many another Italian palace, the stone seat about the base gives scale to the building because the beholder knows instinctively that the height of such a seat must have same relation to the length of a man's leg. In the Pitti palace the balustrade which crowns each story answers a similar purpose: it stands in no intimate relation to the gigantic

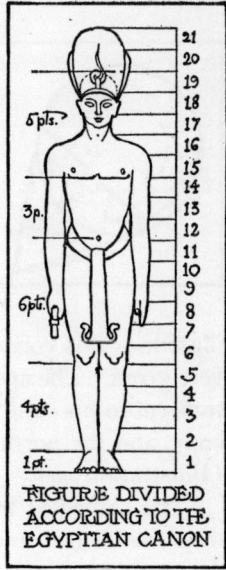

47

FIGURE DIVIDED ACCORDING TO THE EGYPTIAN CANON

48

arches below, but is of a height convenient for lounging elbows. The door to Giotto's campanile reveals the true size of the tower as nothing else could, because it is so evidently related to the human figure and not to the great windows higher up in the shaft.

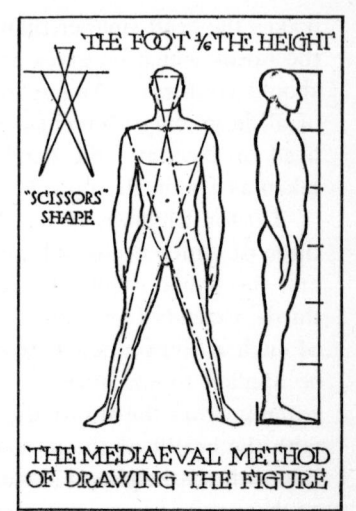

The geometrical plane figures which play the most important part in architectural proportion are the square, the circle and the triangle; and the human figure is intimately related to these elementary forms. If a man stand with heels together, and arms outstretched horizontally in opposite directions, he will be inscribed, as it were, within a square, and his arms will mark, with fair accuracy, the base of an inverted equilateral triangle, the apex of which will touch the ground at his feet. If the arms be extended upward at an angle, and the legs correspondingly separated, the extremities will touch the circumferences of a circle having its center in the navel (Illustrations 45, 46).

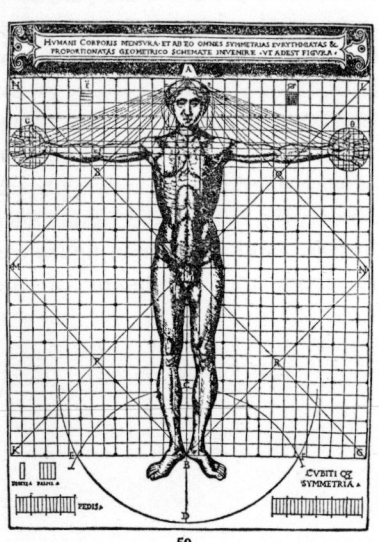

The figure has been variously analyzed with a view to establishing numerical ratios between its parts (Illustrations 47, 48, 49). Some of these are so simple and easily remembered that they have obtained a certain popular currency; such as that the length of the hand equals the length of the face; that the span of the horizontally extended arms equals the height; and the well known rule that twice around the wrist is once around the neck, and twice around the neck is once around the waist. The Roman architect, Vitruvius, writing in the age of Augustus Caesar, formulated the important proportions of the statues of classical antiquity, and except that he makes the head smaller than the normal (as it should be in heroic statuary), the ratios which he gives are those to which the ideally perfect male figure should conform. Among the ancients the foot was probably the standard of all large measurements, being a more determinate length than that of the head or face, and the height was six lengths of the foot. If the head be taken as a unit, the ratio becomes 1:8, and if the face,—1:10.

Doctor Rimmer, in his Art Anatomy, divides the figure into four parts, three of which are equal, and correspond to the lengths of the leg, the thigh and the trunk; while the fourth part, which is two-thirds of one of these thirds, extends from the sternum to the crown of the head. One excellence of such a division aside from its simplicity, consists in the fact that it may be applied to the face as well. The lowest of the three major divisions extends from the tip of the chin to the base of the nose, the next coincides with the height of the nose (its top being level with the eyebrows), and the last with the height of the forehead, while the remaining two-thirds of one of these thirds represents the horizontal projection from the beginning of the hair on the forehead to the crown of the head. The middle of the three larger divisions locates the ears, which are the same height as the nose (Illustration 45).

Such analyses of the figure, however conducted, reveal an all-pervasive harmony of parts, between which definite numerical relations are traceable, and an apprehension of these should assist the architectural designer to arrive at beauty of proportion by methods of his own, not perhaps in the shape of rigid formulae, but present in the consciousness as a restraining influence, acting and reacting upon the mind with a conscious intention towards rhythm and harmony. By means of such exercises, he will approach nearer to an understanding of that great mystery, the beauty and significance of numbers, of which mystery music, architecture, and the human figure are equally presentments—considered, that is, from the standpoint of the occultist.

V

LATENT GEOMETRY

THE analysis of the chemical elements by means of clairvoyant vision, undertaken by Mrs. Besant and Mr. Leadbeater, and lately published to the world in Occult Chemistry, makes plain the fact that units everywhere tend to arrange themselves with relation to certain simple geometrical solids, among which are the tetrahedron, the cube, and the sphere. This process gives rise to harmony, which may be defined as the relation between parts and unity, the simplicity latent in the infinitely complex, the potential complexity of that which is simple. Proceeding to things visible and tangible, this indwelling harmony, rhythm, proportion, which has its basis in geometry and number, is seen to exist in crystals, flower forms, leaf groups, and the like, where it is obvious; and in the more highly organized world of the animal kingdom, also; though here the geometry is latent rather than patent, eluding, though not quite defying analysis, and thus augmenting beauty, which, like a woman, is alluring in proportion as she eludes (Illustrations 51, 52, 53).

By the true artist, in the crystal mirror of whose mind the universal harmony is focused and reflected, this secret of the cause and source of rhythm—that it dwells in a correlation of parts based on an ultimate simplicity—is instinctively apprehended. A knowledge of it formed part of the equipment of the painters who made glorious the golden noon of pictorial art in Italy, during the Renaissance. The problem which preoccupied them was, as Symonds says of Leonardo, "to submit the freest play of form to simple figures of geometry in grouping." Alberti held that the painter should, above all things, have mastered geometry, and it is known that the study of perspective and kindred subjects was widespread and popular.

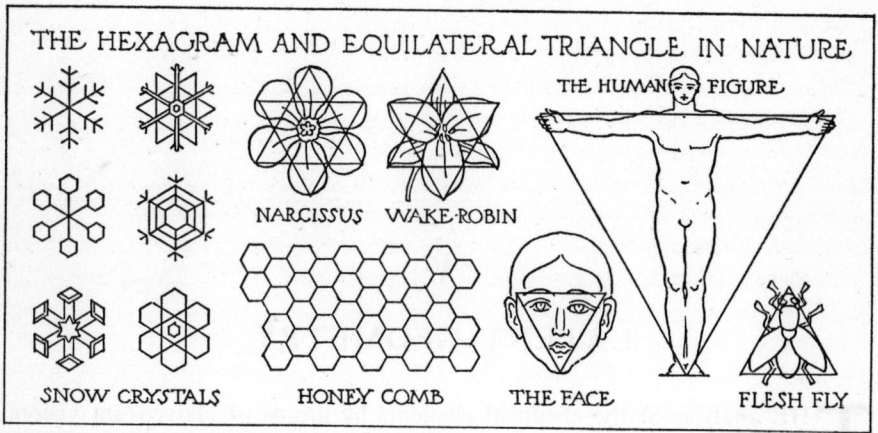

LATENT GEOMETRY

THE HEXAGRAM AND EQUILATERAL TRIANGLE IN NATURE

SNOW CRYSTALS — NARCISSUS — WAKE-ROBIN — THE HUMAN FIGURE — HONEY COMB — THE FACE — FLESH FLY

51

The first painter who deliberately rather than instinctively based his composition on geometrical principles seems to have been Fra Bartolomeo, in his Last Judgment, in the church of St. Maria Nuova, in Florence. Symonds says of this picture, "Simple figures—the pyramid and triangle, upright, inverted, and interwoven like the rhymes of a sonnet—form the basis of the composition. This system was adhered to by the Fratre in all his subsequent works" (Illustration 54). Raphael, with that power of assimilation which distinguishes him among men of genius, learned from Fra Bartolomeo this method of disposing figures and combining them in masses with almost mathematical precision. It would have been indeed surprising if Leonardo da Vinci, in whom the artist and the man of science were so wonderfully united, had not been greatly preoccupied with the mathematics of the art of painting. His Madonna of the Rocks, and Virgin on the

PROPORTIONS OF THE HORSE

52

53

Lap of Saint Anne, in the Louvre, exhibit the very perfection of pyramidal composition. It is, however, in his masterpiece, The Last Supper, that he combines geometrical symmetry and precision with perfect naturalness and freedom in the grouping of individually interesting and dramatic figures. Michael Angelo, Andrea del Sarto, and the great Venetians, in whose work the art of painting may be said to have culminated, recognized and obeyed those mathematical laws of composition known to their immediate predecessors, and the decadence of the art in the ensuing period may be traced not alone to the false sentiment and affectation of the times, but also in the abandonment by the artists of those obscurely geometrical arrangements and groupings which, in the works of the greatest masters, so satisfy the eye and haunt the memory of the beholder (Illustrations 55, 56).

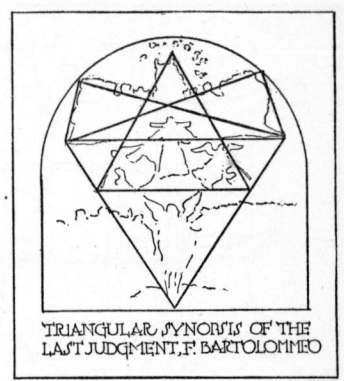

Sculpture, even more than painting, is based on geometry. The colossi of Egypt, the bas-reliefs of Assyria, the figured pediments and metopes of the temples of Greece, the carved tombs of Ravenna, the Della Robbia lunettes, the sculptured tympani of Gothic church portals,

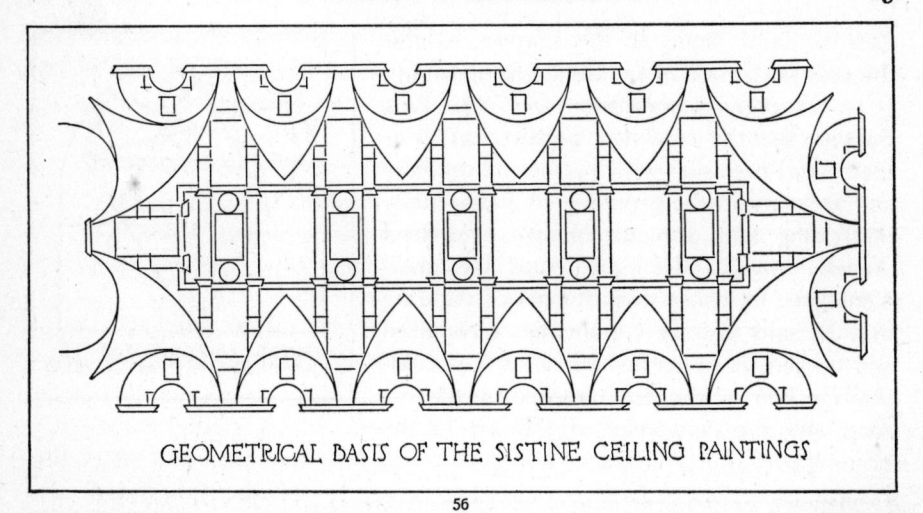

GEOMETRICAL BASIS OF THE SISTINE CEILING PAINTINGS

56

all alike lend themselves in greater or less degree to a geometrical synopsis (Illustration 57). Whenever sculpture suffered divorce from architecture, the geometrical element became less prominent, doubtless because of all the arts architecture is the most clearly and closely related to geometry. Indeed, it may be said that architecture is geometry made visible, in the same sense that music is number made audible. A building is an aggregation of the commonest geometrical forms: parallelograms, prisms, pyramids, and cones,—the cylinder appearing in the column, and the hemisphere in the dome. The plans, likewise, of the world's famous buildings, reduced to their simplest expression, are discovered to resolve themselves into a few simple geometrical figures (Illustration 58).

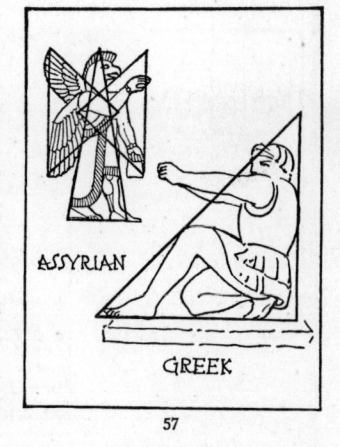

But architecture is geometrical in another and a higher sense than this. Emerson says: "The pleasure a palace or a temple gives the eye is that an order and a method has been communicated to stones, so that they speak and geometrize, become tender or sublime with expression." All truly great and beautiful works of architecture—from the Egyptian pyramids to the cathedrals of the Ile-de-France—are harmoniously proportioned, their principal and subsidiary masses being related, sometimes obviously, more often obscurely, to certain symmetrical figures of geometry, which, though invisible to the sight, and not consciously present in the mind of the beholder, yet perform the important function of co-ordinating the entire fabric into one easily remembered whole. Upon some such principle is surely founded what Symonds calls "that severe and lofty art of composition which seeks the highest beauty of design in architectural harmony supreme, above the melodies of gracefulness of detail."

There is abundant evidence in support of the theory that the builders of antiquity, the masonic guilds of the Middle Ages, and the architects of the Italian Renaissance, knew and followed certain rules; but though this theory be denied, or even disproven, if after all these men obtained their results

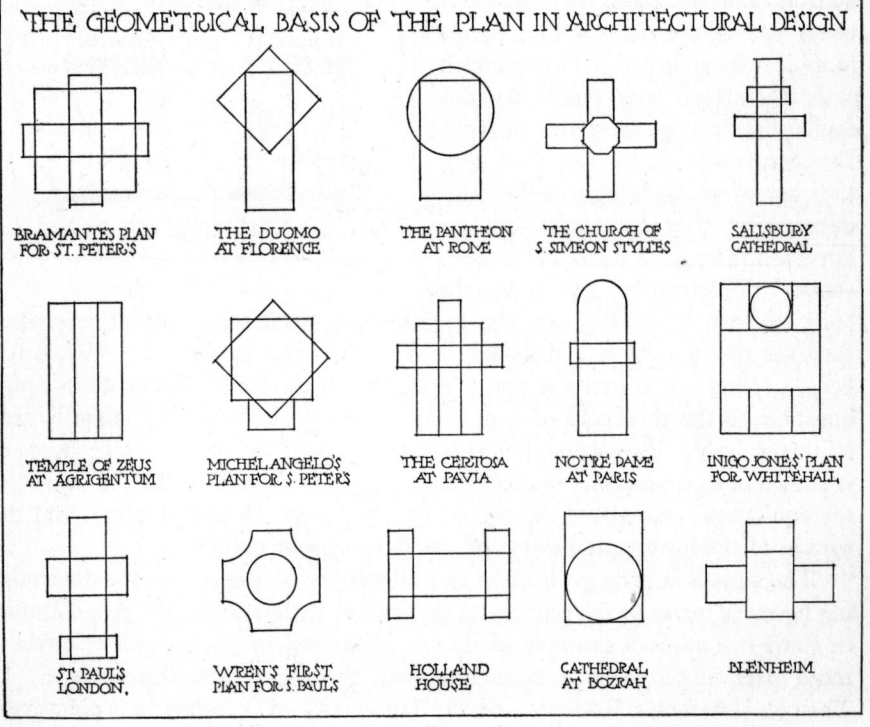

THE GEOMETRICAL BASIS OF THE PLAN IN ARCHITECTURAL DESIGN

BRAMANTE'S PLAN FOR ST. PETER'S — THE DUOMO AT FLORENCE — THE PANTHEON AT ROME — THE CHURCH OF S. SIMEON STYLITES — SALISBURY CATHEDRAL

TEMPLE OF ZEUS AT AGRIGENTUM — MICHELANGELO'S PLAN FOR S. PETER'S — THE CERTOSA AT PAVIA — NOTRE DAME AT PARIS — INIGO JONES' PLAN FOR WHITEHALL

ST. PAUL'S LONDON — WREN'S FIRST PLAN FOR S. PAUL'S — HOLLAND HOUSE — CATHEDRAL AT BOZRAH — BLENHEIM

58

unconsciously, their creations so lend themselves to a geometrical analysis that the claim for the existence of certain canons of proportion, based on geometry, remains unimpeached.

The plane figures principally employed in determining architectural proportion are the circle, the equilateral triangle, and the square—which also yields the right angled isosceles triangle. It will be noted that these are the two-dimensional correlatives of the sphere, the tetrahedron, and the cube, mentioned as being among the determining forms in molecular structure. The question naturally arises, why the circle, the equilateral triangle and the square? Because, aside from the fact that they are of all plane figures the most elementary, they are intimately related to the body of man, as has been shown (Illustration 45), and the body of man is, as it were, the architectural archetype. But this simply removes the inquiry to a different field, it does not answer it. Why is the body of man so constructed and related? This leads us, as does every question, to the threshold of a mystery upon which theosophy alone is able to throw light. Any extended elucidation would be out of place here: it is sufficient to remind the reader that the circle is the symbol of the universe, the equilateral triangle of the higher trinity (*atma, buddhi, manas*), and the square of the lower quatrinary, of man's sevenfold nature.

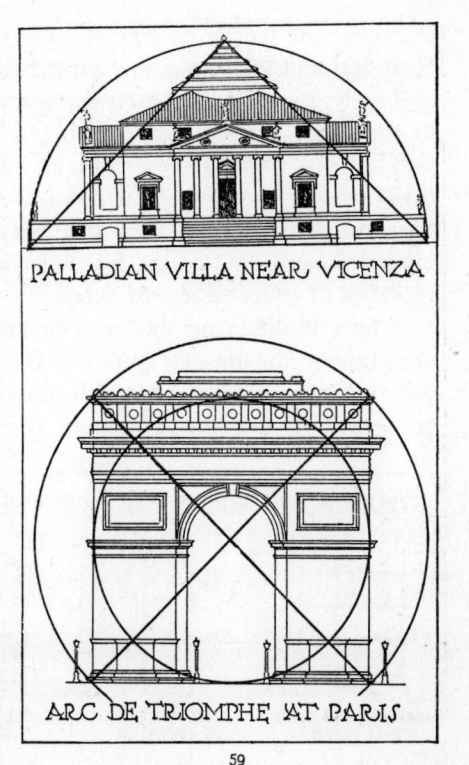

The square is principally used in preliminary plotting: it is the determining figure in many of the palaces of the Italian Renaissance; the Arc d'Etoille in Paris is a modern example of its use (Illustrations 59, 60). The circle is most often employed in conjunction with the square and the triangle. In Thomas Jefferson's Rotunda for the University of Virginia, a single great circle was the determining figure, as his original pen sketch of the building shows. Some of the best Roman triumphal arches submit themselves to a circular synopsis, and a system of double intersecting circles has been applied, with interesting results, to façades as widely different as those of the Parthenon and the Farnese Palace in Rome, though it would be fatuous to claim that these figures determined the proportions of these façades.

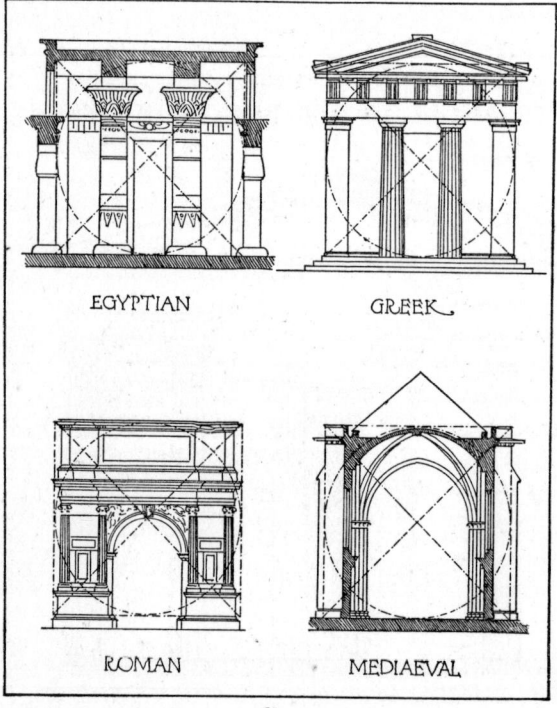

By far the most important figure in architectural proportion, considered from the standpoint of geometry, is the equilateral triangle. It would seem that the eye has an especial fondness for this figure, just as the ear has, for certain related sounds. Indeed, it might not be too fanciful to assert that the common chord of any key (the tonic with its third and fifth) is the musical equivalent of the equilateral triangle. It is scarcely necessary to dwell upon the properties and unique perfection of this figure. Of all regular polygons it is the simplest; its three equal sides subtend equal angles, each of 60 degrees; it trisects the circumference of a circle; it is the graphic symbol of the number three, and hence of every three-fold thing; doubled, its

V   LATENT GEOMETRY

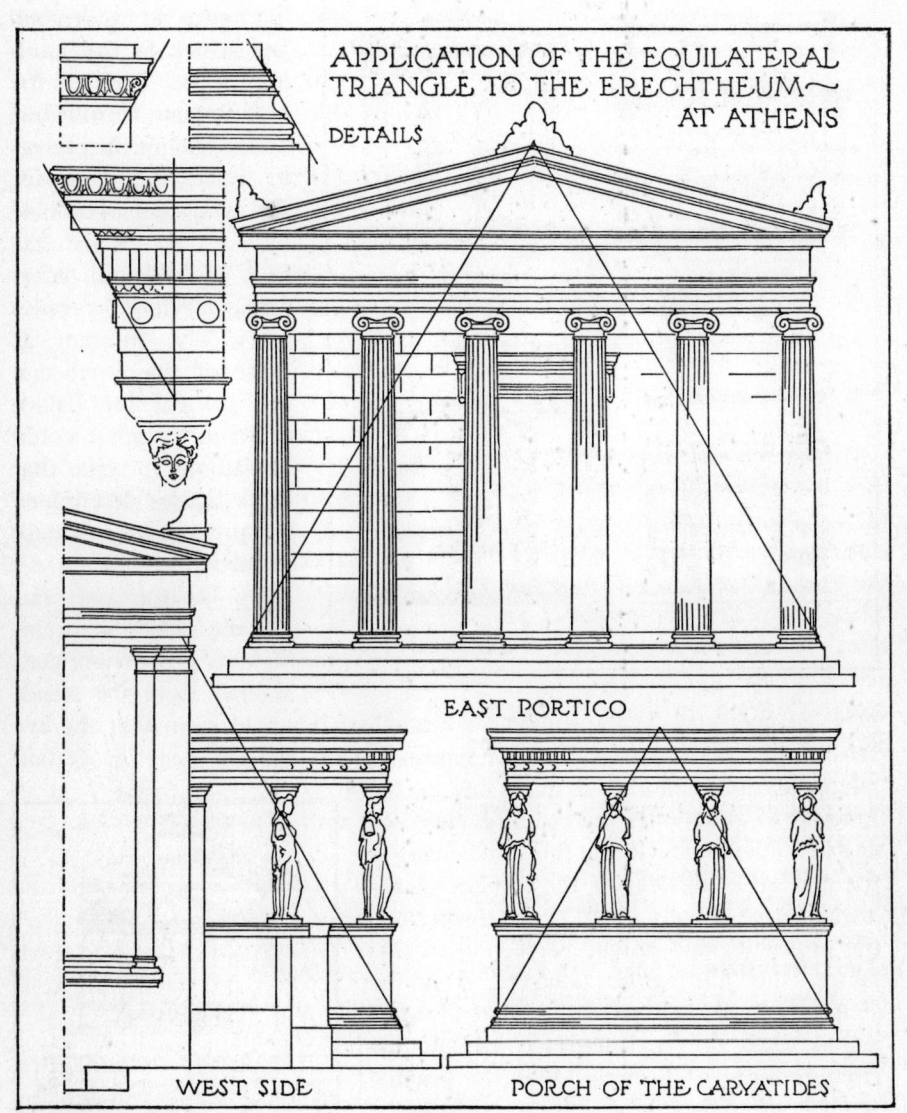

APPLICATION OF THE EQUILATERAL TRIANGLE TO THE ERECHTHEUM AT ATHENS

DETAILS

EAST PORTICO

WEST SIDE   PORCH OF THE CARYATIDES

generating arcs form the *vesica piscis,* of so frequent occurrence in early Christian art; two symmetrically intersecting equilateral triangles yield the figure known as "Solomon's Seal," or the "Shield of David," to which mystic properties have always been ascribed.

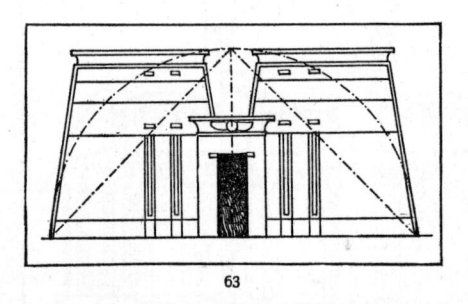

63

It may be stated as a general rule that whenever three important points in any architectural composition coincide (approximately or exactly) with the three extremities of an equilateral triangle, it makes for beauty of proportion. An ancient and notable example occurs in the pyramids of Egypt, the sides of which, in their original condition, are believed to have been equilateral triangles. It is a demonstrable fact that certain geometrical intersections yield the important proportions of Greek architecture. The perfect little Erechtheum would seem to have been proportioned by means of the equilateral triangle and the angle of 60 degrees, both in general and in detail (Illustration 62). The same angle, erected from the central axis of a column at the point where it intersects the architrave, determines both the projection of the cornice and the

THE EQUILATERAL TRIANGLE IN ROMAN ARCHITECTURE

ARCH OF TITUS, ROME

ARCH OF CONSTANTINE, ROME

A SECTION OF THE PANTHEON, ROME

64

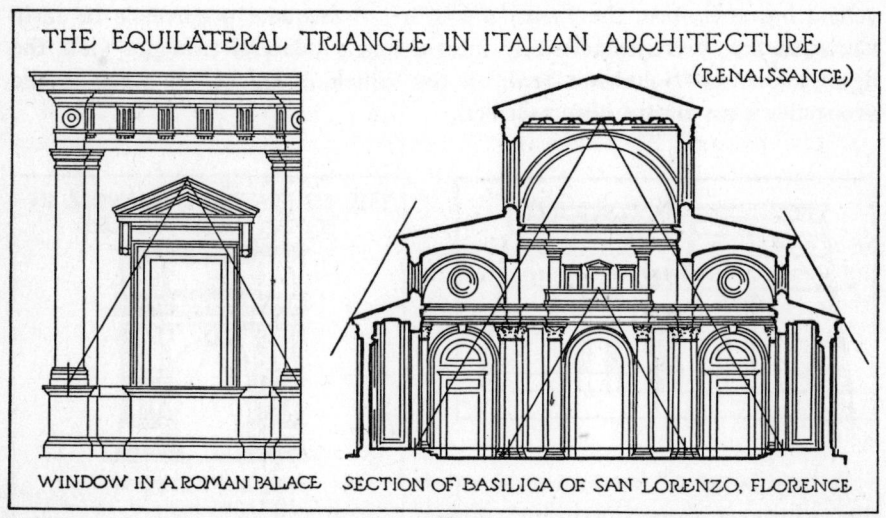

THE EQUILATERAL TRIANGLE IN ITALIAN ARCHITECTURE
(RENAISSANCE)

WINDOW IN A ROMAN PALACE SECTION OF BASILICA OF SAN LORENZO, FLORENCE

65

height of the architrave, in many of the finest Greek and Roman temples (Illustrations 67-70). The equilateral triangle used in conjunction with the circle and the square was employed by the Romans in determining the proportions of triumphal arches, basilicas and baths. That the same figure was a factor in the designing of Gothic cathedrals is sufficiently indicated in the accompanying facsimile reproduction of an illustration from the Como Vitruvius, published in Milan in 1521, which shows a vertical section of the Milan cathedral and the system of equilateral triangles which determined its various parts (Illustration 71). The *vesica piscis* was often used to establish the two main internal dimensions of the cathedral plan; the greatest diameter of the figure corresponding with the width across the transepts, the upper apex marking the limit of the apse, and the lower, the termination of the nave. Such a proportion is seen to be both subtle and simple, and possesses the advantage of being easily laid out. The architects of the Italian Renaissance doubtless inherited certain of the Roman canons of architectural proportion, for they seem very generally to have recognized them as an essential principle of design.

Nevertheless, when all is said, it is easy to exaggerate the importance of this matter of geometrical proportion. The designer who seeks the ultimate secret of architectural harmony in mathematics rather than in the trained eye, is following the wrong road to success. A happy inspiration is worth all the formulas in the world—if it is really happy, the artist will probably find that he has "followed the rules without knowing them." Even while formulating concepts of art the author must again reiterate that the concept is unfruitful in art. The "mechanism" of spatial beauty is an interesting study, and within certain limits, a useful one; but it can never take the place of the creative faculty, it can only restrain and direct it. The study of proportion is to the architect what the study of harmony is to a musician,—it helps his genius adequately to express itself.

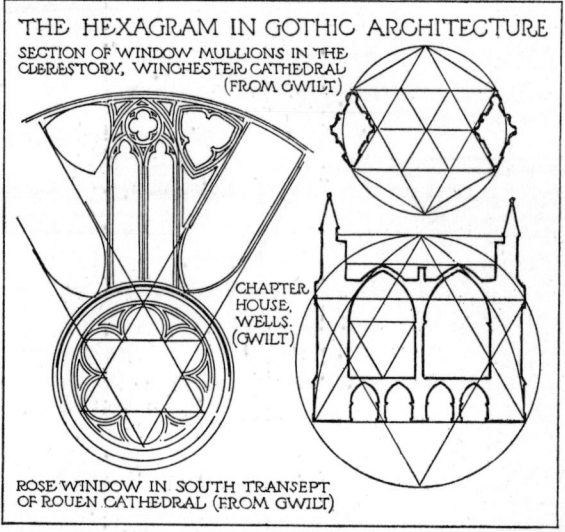

THE HEXAGRAM IN GOTHIC ARCHITECTURE

SECTION OF WINDOW MULLIONS IN THE CLERESTORY, WINCHESTER CATHEDRAL (FROM GWILT)

CHAPTER HOUSE, WELLS. (GWILT)

ROSE WINDOW IN SOUTH TRANSEPT OF ROUEN CATHEDRAL (FROM GWILT)

V   LATENT GEOMETRY   71

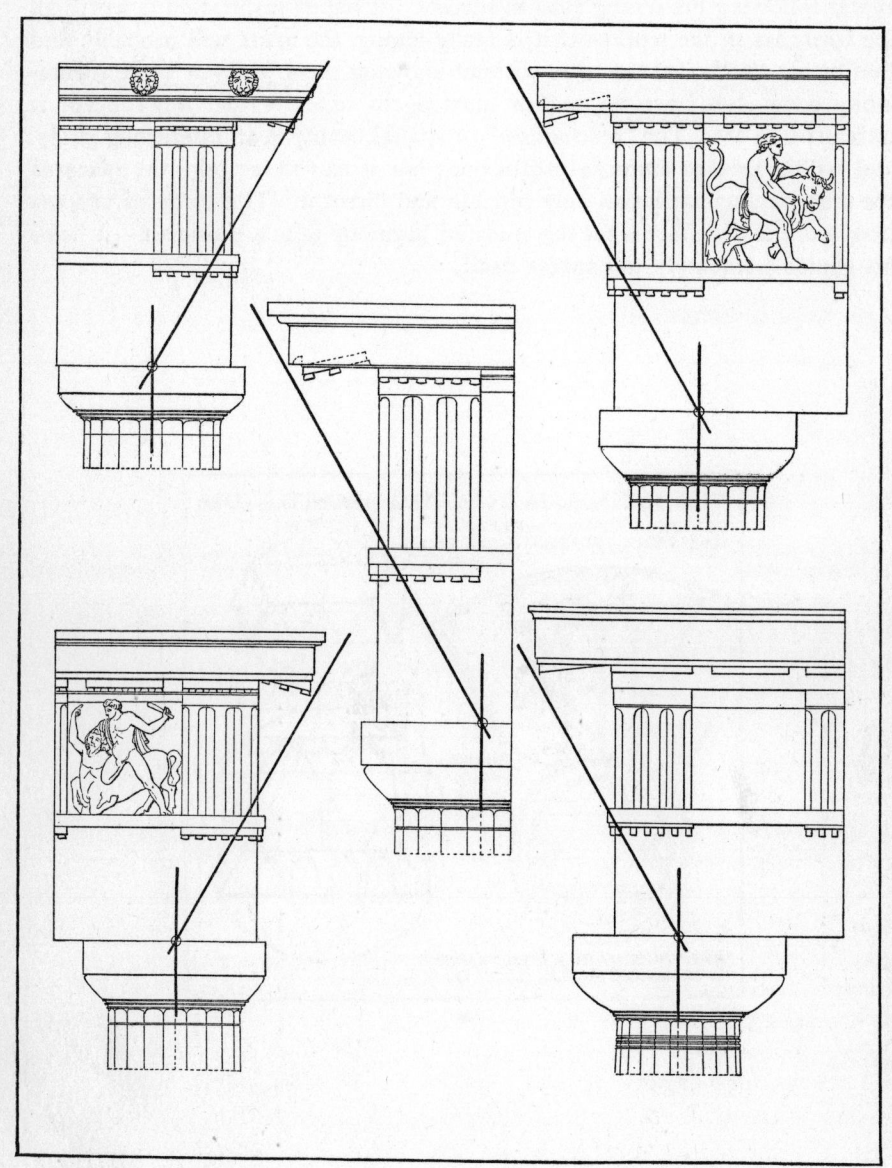

67

72 THE BEAUTIFUL NECESSITY V

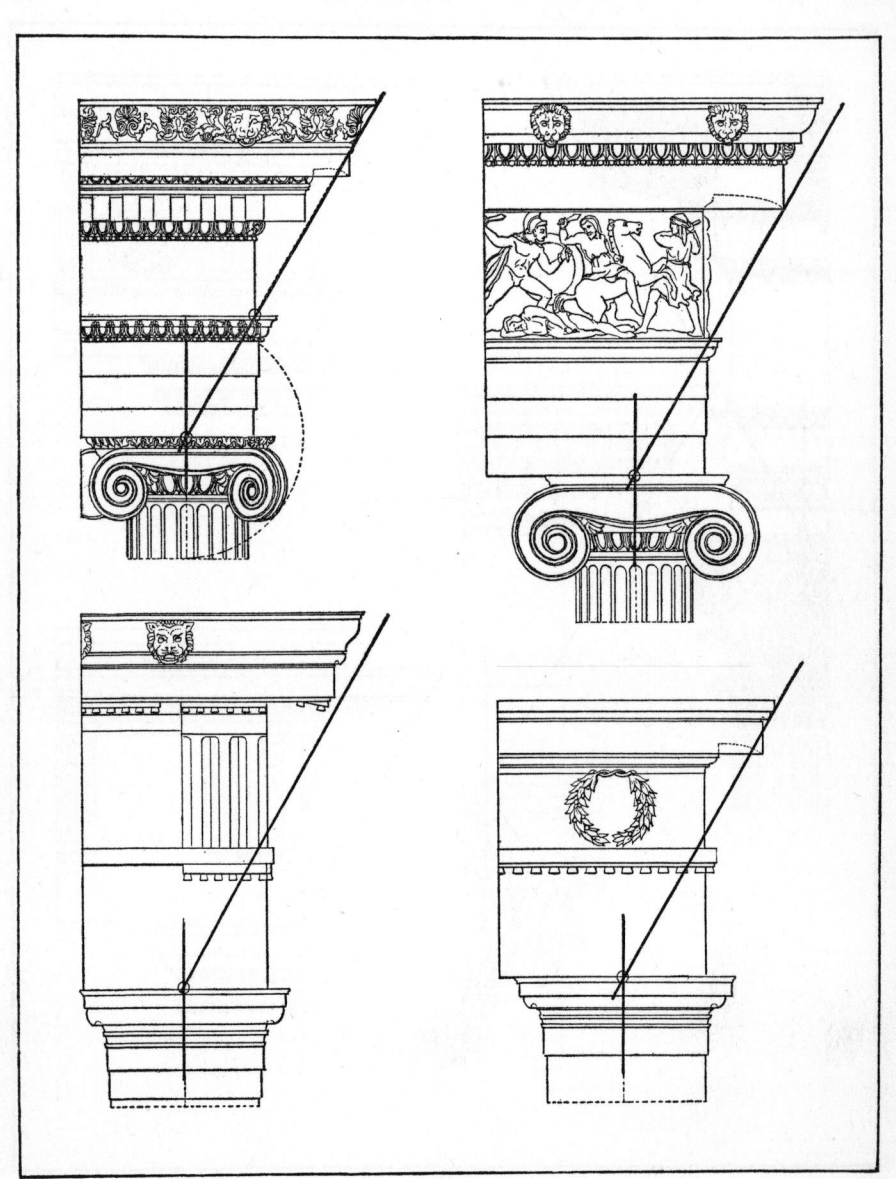

V LATENT GEOMETRY 73

74 THE BEAUTIFUL NECESSITY V

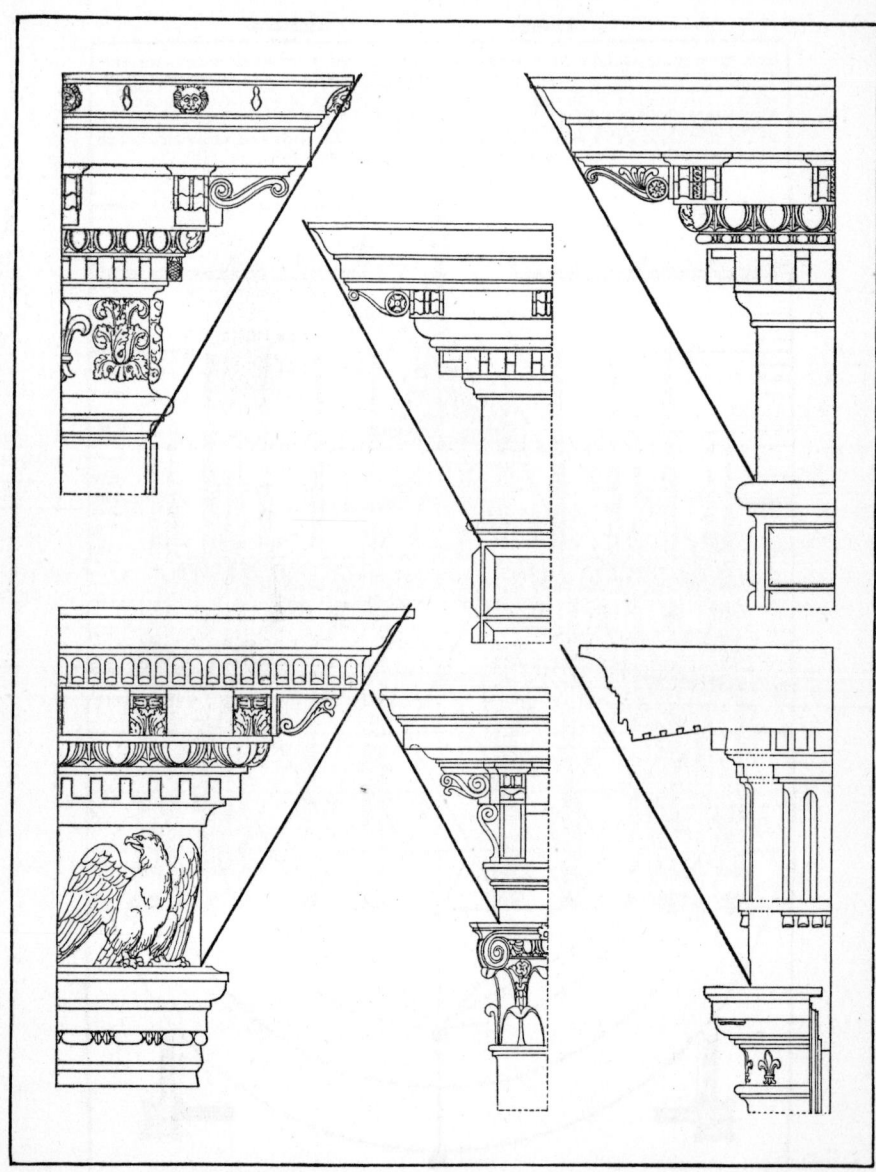

LATENT GEOMETRY

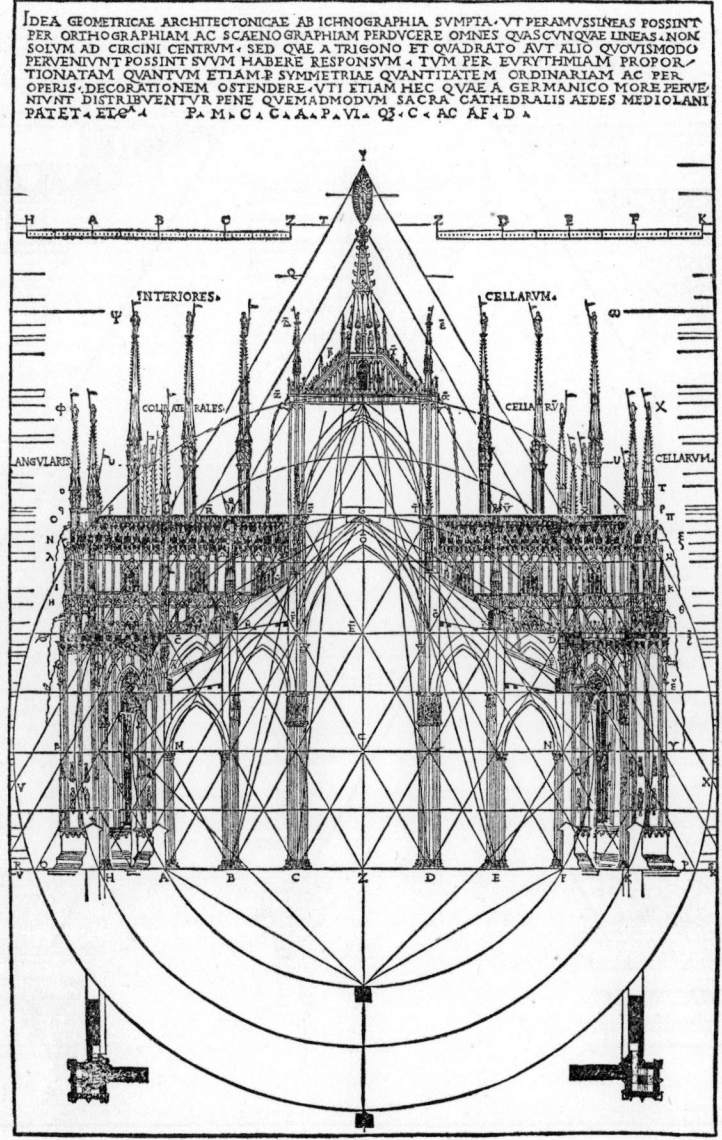

LIBER PRIMVS

IDEA GEOMETRICAE ARCHITECTONICAE AB ICHNOGRAPHIA SVMPTA · VT PER AMVSSI NEAS POSSINT PER ORTHOGRAPHIAM AC SCAENOGRAPHIAM PERDVCERE OMNES QVASCVNQVAE LINEAS · NON SOLVM AD CIRCINI CENTRVM · SED QVAE A TRIGONO ET QVADRATO AVT ALIO QVOVISMODO PERVENIVNT POSSINT SVVM HABERE RESPONSVM · TVM PER EVRYTHMIAM PROPORTIONATAM QVANTVM ETIAM P. SYMMETRIAE QVANTITATEM ORDINARIAM AC PER OPERIS · DECORATIONEM OSTENDERE · VTI ETIAM HEC QVAE A GERMANICO MORE PERVENIVNT DISTRIBVENTVR PENE QVEMADMODVM SACRA CATHEDRALIS AEDES MEDIOLANI PATET · ETC^A ·   P · M · C · A · A · P · VI · Q3 · C · AC · AF · D ·

71

VI

THE ARITHMETIC OF BEAUTY

ALTHOUGH architecture is based primarily upon geometry, it is possible to express all spatial relations numerically, for arithmetic, and not geometry, is the universal science of quantity. The relation of masses one to another—of voids to solids, and of heights and lengths to widths—form ratios; and when such ratios are simple and harmonious, architecture may be said, in Walter Pater's famous phrase, to "aspire towards the condition of music." The trained eye, and not an arithmetical formula, determines what is, and what is not, beautiful proportion. Nevertheless the fact that the eye instinctively rejects certain proportions as unpleasing, and accepts others as satisfactory, is an indication of the existence of spatial laws based upon number, not unlike those which govern musical harmony. The secret of the deep reasonableness of such selection by the senses lies hidden in the very nature of number itself, for number is the invisible thread on which the worlds are strung—the universe abstractly symbolized.

Number is the *within* of all things,—the "first form of Brahman." It is the measure of time and space; it lurks in the heart beat and is blazoned upon the starred canopy of night. Substance, in a state of vibration, that is, conditioned by number, ceaselessly undergoes the myriad transmutations which produce phenomenal life. Elements separate and combine chemically according to numerical ratios: "Moon, plant, gas, crystal are concrete geometry and number." By the Pythagoreans and by the ancient Egyptians sex was attributed to numbers, odd numbers being conceived of as masculine, or generating, and even numbers as feminine, or parturitive, on account of

THE ARITHMETIC OF BEAUTY

their infinite divisibility. Harmonious combinations were those involving the marriage of a masculine and a feminine—an odd and an even—number.

Number proceeds from unity towards infinity, and returns again to unity as the soul, defined by Pythagoras as a self-moving number, goes forth from, and returns to God. These two acts, one of projection, and the other of recall; these two forces, centrifugal and centripetal, are symbolized in the operations of addition and subtraction. Within them is embraced the whole of computation; but because every number, every aggregation of units, is also a new unit capable of being added or subtracted, there are also the operations of multiplication and division, which consist, in the one case, of the addition of several equal numbers together, and in the other, of the subtraction of several equal numbers from a greater until that is exhausted.

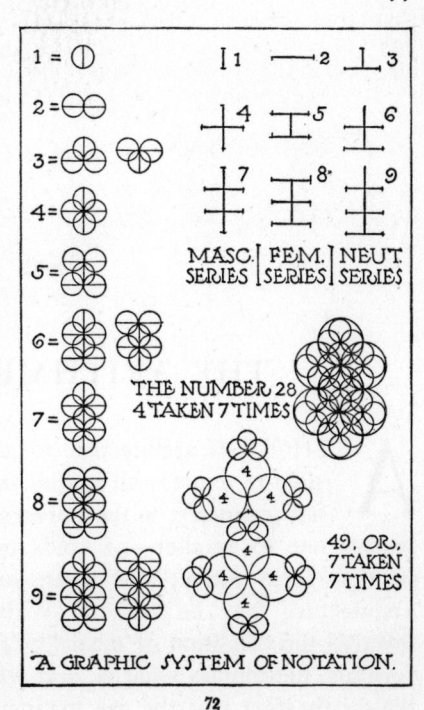

The progression and retrogression of numbers in groups expressed by the multiplication table gives rise to what may be termed "numerical conjunctions." These are analogous to astronomical conjunctions: the planets, revolving around the sun at different rates of speed, and in widely separated orbits, at certain times come into line with each other and with the sun. They are then said to be in conjunction. Similarly, numbers, advancing towards infinity singly and in groups (expressed by the multiplication table), at certain stages of their progression come into relation with one another. For example, an important conjunction occurs in 12, for of a

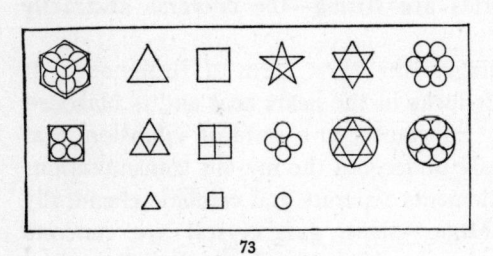

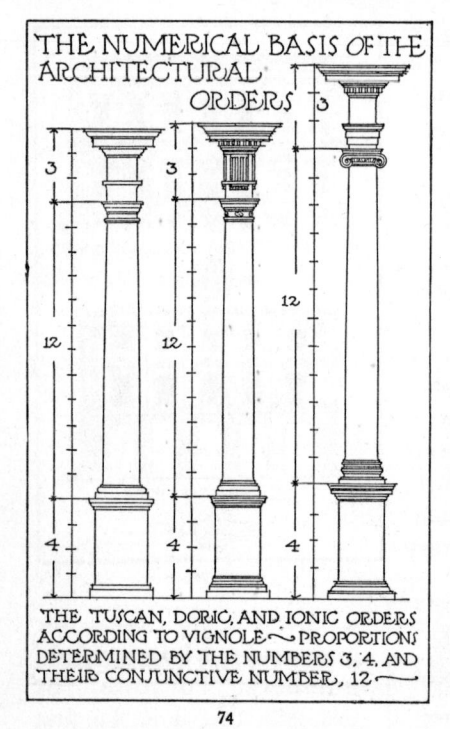

THE NUMERICAL BASIS OF THE ARCHITECTURAL ORDERS

THE TUSCAN, DORIC, AND IONIC ORDERS ACCORDING TO VIGNOLE — PROPORTIONS DETERMINED BY THE NUMBERS 3, 4, AND THEIR CONJUNCTIVE NUMBER, 12

series of twos it is the sixth, of threes the fourth, of fours the third, and of sixes the second. It stands to 8 in the ratio of 3:2, and to 9 of 4:3. It is related to 7 through being the product of 3 and 4, of which numbers 7 is the sum. Eleven and thirteen are not conjunctive numbers. Fourteen is so in the series of twos, fours, and sevens; 15 is so in the series of fives and threes. The next conjunction after 12, of 3 and 4 and their first multiples, is in 24, and the next following is 36, which numbers are respectively the two and three of a series of twelves, each end being but a new beginning.

It will be seen that this discovery of numerical conjunctions consists merely of resolving numbers into their prime factors, and that a conjunctive number is a common multiple; but by naming it so, to dismiss the entire subject as known and exhausted, is to miss a sense of the wonder, beauty, and rhythm of it all, a mental impression analogous to that made upon the

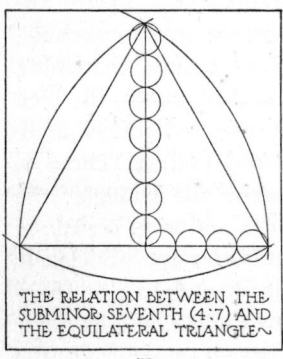

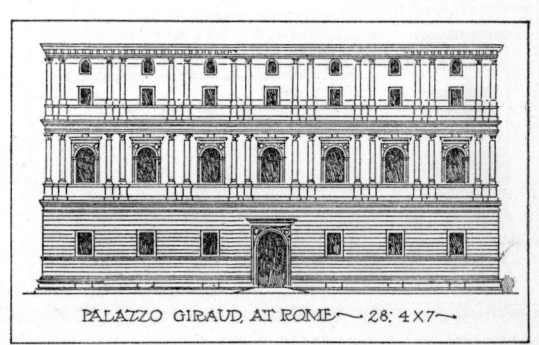

THE RELATION BETWEEN THE SUBMINOR SEVENTH (4:7) AND THE EQUILATERAL TRIANGLE

PALAZZO GIRAUD, AT ROME — 28: 4×7

VI THE ARITHMETIC OF BEAUTY

eye by the swift glancing balls of a juggler, the evolutions of drilling troops, or the intricate figures of a dance, for these things are number concrete and animate in time and space.

The truths of number are of all truths the most interior, abstract, and difficult of apprehension, and since knowledge becomes clear and definite to the extent that it can be made to enter the mind through the channels of physical sense, it is well to accustom oneself to conceiving of number graphically, by means of geometrical symbols (Illustration 72), rather than in terms of the familiar Arabic notation which, though admirable for purposes of computation, is of too condensed and arbitrary a character to reveal the properties of individual numbers. To state, for example, that 4 is the first square, and 8 the first cube, conveys but a vague idea to most persons, but if 4 be represented as a square enclosing four smaller squares, and 8 as a cube containing eight smaller cubes, the idea is apprehended immediately and without effort. Three is, of course, the triangle; the irregular and vital beauty of the number 5 appears clearly in the heptalpha, or five-pointed star; the faultless symmetry of 6, its relation to 3 and 2, and its regular division of the circle, are portrayed in the familiar hexagram known as the

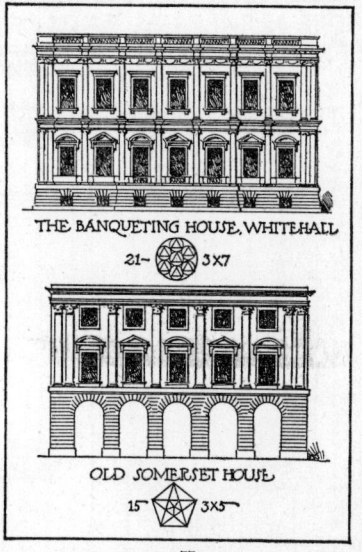

THE BROLETTA AT MANTUA | PALAZZO UGUCCIONI AT FLORENCE

PALAZZO BARTOLINI, FLORENCE | PALAZZO TACCONI, BOLOGNA
VARIOUS PALACE FAÇADES ~ 3 USED AS A MULTIPLE

Shield of David. Seven, when represented as a compact group of circles, reveals itself as a number of singular beauty and perfection worthy of the important place accorded to it in all mystical philosophy. It is a curious fact that when asked to think of any number less than 10, most persons will choose 7 (Illustration 73).

Every form of art, though primarily a vehicle for the expression and transmission of particular ideas and emotions, has subsidiary offices, just as a musical tone has harmonics which render it more sweet. Painting reveals the nature of color; music, of sound in wood, in brass, and in stretched strings; architecture shows forth the qualities of light, and the strength and beauty of materials. All of the arts, and particularly music and architecture, portray in different manners and degrees the truths of number. Architecture does this in two ways: esoterically, as it were, in the form of harmonic proportions; and exoterically in the form of symbols which represent numbers and groups of numbers. The fact that a series of threes and a series of fours mutually conjoin in 12, finds an architectural expression in the Tuscan, the Doric, and the Ionic orders according to Vignole, for in them all the stylobate is four parts, the entablature 3, and the intermediate column 12 (Illustration 74). The affinity between 4 and 7, revealed in the fact that they express the ratio between the base and the altitude of the right-angled triangle which forms half of an equilateral, and the musical intervals of the diminished seventh (Illustration 75) is architecturally suggested in the Palazzo Giraud, which is four stories in height with seven openings in each story (Illustration 76).

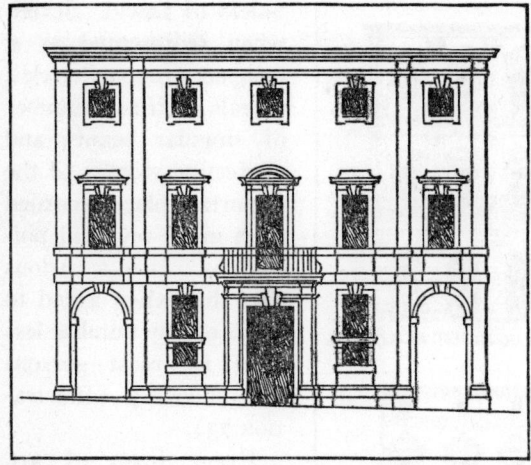

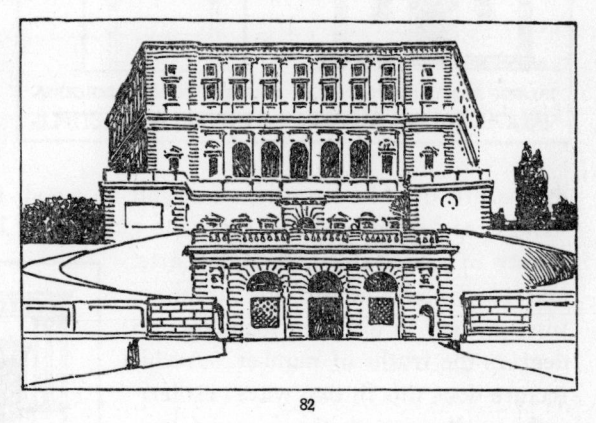

Every building is a symbol of some number or group of numbers, and other things being equal the more perfect the numbers involved the more beautiful will be the building (Illustrations 77-83). Three, 5, and 7—the numbers which occur oftenest—are the most satisfactory because, being of small quantity, they are easily grasped by the eye, and being odd, they yield a center or axis, so necessary in every architectural composition. Next in value are the lowest multiples of these numbers and the least common multiples of any two of them, because the eye, with a little assistance, is able to resolve them into their constituent factors. It is part of the art of architecture to render such assistance, for the eye counts always, consciously or unconsciously, and when it is confronted with a number of units greater than it can readily resolve, it is refreshed and rested if these units are so grouped and arranged that they reveal themselves as factors of some higher quantity.

There is a raison d'etre for string courses other than to mark the position of a floor on the interior of a building, and for quoins and pilasters other than to indicate the presence of a transverse wall. These sometimes serve the useful purpose of so subdividing a façade that the eye estimates the number of its openings without conscious effort and consequent fatigue (Illustration 83). The tracery of Gothic rose-windows forms perhaps the highest and finest architectural expression of number (Illustration 84). Just as thirst makes water more sweet, so does Gothic tracery confuse the eye with its complexity only the more greatly to gratify the sight by revealing the inherent simplicity in which this complexity has its root. Sometimes, as in the case of the Venetian Ducal Palace, the numbers involved are too great for counting, but other and different arithmetical truths are portrayed; for example, the multiplication of the first arcade by 2 in the second, and this by 3 in the cusped arches,

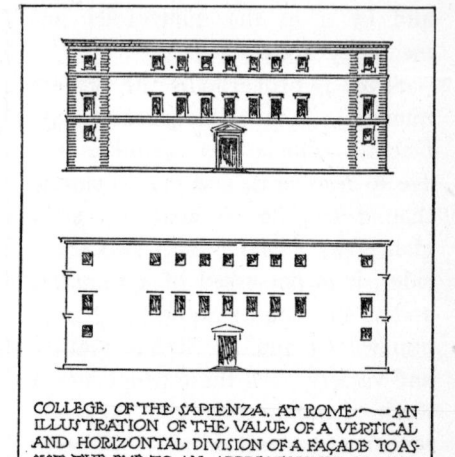

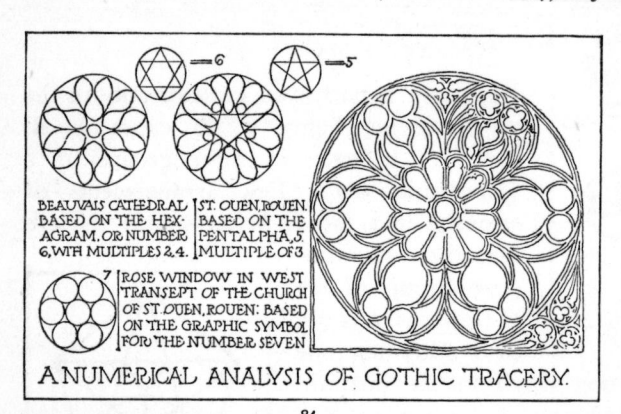

VI THE ARITHMETIC OF BEAUTY

and by 4 in the quatrefoils immediately above.

Seven is proverbially the perfect number. It is of a quantity sufficiently complex to stimulate the eye to resolve it, and yet so simple that it can be so analyzed at a glance; as a center with two equal sides, it is possessed of symmetry, and as the sum of an odd and even number (3 and 4), it has vitality and variety. All these properties a work of architecture can variously reveal (Illustration 78). Fifteen, also, is a number of great perfection. It is possible to arrange the first 9 numbers in the form of a "magic" square so that the sum of each line, read across or up or down, will be 15. Thus:

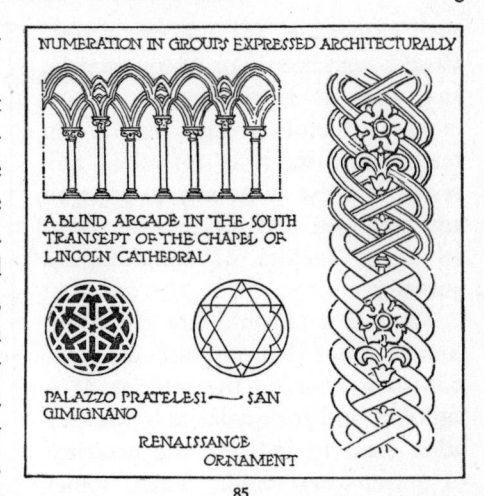

4	9	2	=	15
3	5	7	=	15
8	1	6	=	15
15	15	15		

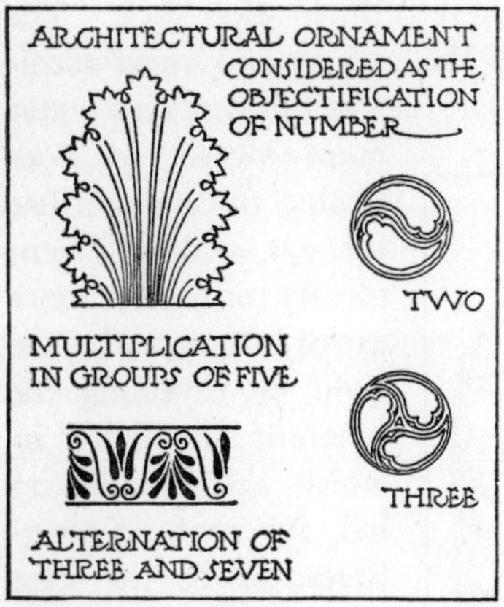

Its beauty is portrayed geometrically in the accompanying figure which expresses it, being 15 triangles in three groups of 5 (Illustration 87). Few arrangements of openings in a façade better satisfy the eye than three superimposed groups of five (Illustrations 77, 81). May not one source of this satisfaction dwell in the intrinsic beauty of the number 15?

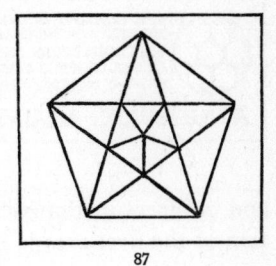

In conclusion, it is perhaps well that the reader be again reminded that these are the by-ways, and not the highways of architecture: that the highest beauty comes always, not from beautiful numbers, nor from likenesses to Nature's eternal patterns of the world, but from utility, fitness, economy, and the perfect adaptation of means to ends. But along with this truth there goes another: that in every excellent work of architecture, in addition to its obvious and individual beauty, there dwells an esoteric and universal beauty, following as it does, the archetypal pattern laid down by the Great Architect for the building of that temple which is the world wherein we dwell.

VII

FROZEN MUSIC

IN the series of essays of which this is the final one, the author has undertaken to enforce the truth that evolution on any plane and on any scale proceeds according to certain laws which are in reality only ramifications of one ubiquitous and ever operative law; that this law registers itself in the thing evolved, leaving stamped thereon, as it were, fossil footprints by means of which it may be known. In the arts the creative spirit of man is at its freest and finest and nowhere among the arts is it so free and so fine as in music. In music, accordingly, the universal law of becoming finds instant, direct, and perfect self-expression; music voices the inner nature of the *will-to-live* in all its moods and moments; in it, form, content, means and end, are perfectly fused. It is this fact which gives validity to the before quoted saying that all of the arts "aspire towards the condition of music." All aspire to express the law, but music, being unincumbered by the leaden burden of gross physical matter, expresses it most easily and adequately. This being so, there is nothing unreasonable in attempting to apply the known facts of musical harmony and rhythm to any other art, and since these essays concern themselves primarily with architecture, the final aspect in which that art will be presented here is as "frozen music"—ponderable matter governed by musical law.

Music depends primarily upon the equal and regular division of time into beats, and of these beats into measures. Over this soundless and invisible warp is woven an infinitely various melodic pattern, made up of tones of different pitch and duration arithmetically related and combined, according to the laws of harmony. Architecture, correspondingly, implies the rhythmical division of space, and obedience to laws numerical and geometrical. A certain identity, therefore, exists between simple harmony in music, and simple proportion in architecture. By translating the consonant tone intervals into number, the common denominator, as it were, of both arts, it is possible to give these intervals a spatial, and hence an architectural expression. Such expression, considered as proportion only and divorced from ornament, will prove pleasing to the eye in the same way that its correlative is pleasing to the ear, because in either case it is not alone the special organ of sense which is gratified, but that inner Self, in which all senses are one. Containing within Itself the mystery of number, It thrills responsive to every audible or visible presentment of that mystery.

THE NORMAN PORCH CANTERBURY~ AN ARCHITECTURAL EXPRESSION OF A NOTE & HARMONICS

If a vibrating string yielding a certain musical note be stopped in its center, that is, divided by half, it will then sound the octave of that note. The numerical ratio which expresses the interval of the octave is therefore 1:2. If one-third instead of one-half of the string be stopped, and the remaining two-thirds struck, it will yield the musical fifth of the original note, which thus corresponds to the ratio 2:3. The length represented by 3:4 yields the fourth; 4:5 the major third; and 5:6 the minor third. These comprise the principal consonant intervals within the scope of one octave. The ratios of inverted intervals, so called, are found by doubling the smaller number of the original interval as given above. 2:3, the fifth, gives 3:4, the fourth; 4:5, the major third, gives 5:8, the minor sixth; 5:6, the minor third, gives 6:10, or 3:5, the major sixth.

Of these various consonant intervals the octave, fifth, and major third are the most important, in the sense of being the most perfect, and they are expressed by numbers of the smallest quantity, an odd number and an even. It will be noted that all of the intervals above given are expressed by the numbers 1, 2, 3, 4, 5 and 6, except the minor sixth (5:8), and this is the most imperfect of all consonant intervals. The sub-minor seventh, expressed by the ratio 4:7, though included among the dissonances, forms, according to Helmholtz, a more perfect consonance with the tonic than the minor sixth.

A natural deduction from these facts is that relations of architectural length and breadth, heighth and width, to be "musical" should be capable of being expressed by ratios of quantitively small numbers, preferably an odd number and an even. Although, generally speaking, the simpler the ratio the more perfect the consonance, yet the intervals of the fifth and major third (2:3 and 4:5), are considered to be more pleasing than the octave (1:2), which is too obviously a repetition of the original note. From this it is reasonable to assume (and the assumption is borne out by experience), that proportions the numerical ratios of which the eye resolves too readily become at last wearisome. The relation should be felt rather than fathomed. There should be a perception of identity, and also of difference. As in music, where dissonances are introduced, to give value to consonances which follow them, so in architecture simple ratios should be employed in connection with those more complex.

Harmonics are those tones which sound with and re-enforce any musical note when it is sounded. The distinguishable harmonics of the tonic yield the ratios 1:2, 2:3, 3:4, 4:5 and 4:7. A note and its harmonics form a natural chord. They may be compared to the widening circles which appear in still water when a stone is dropped into it, for when a musical sound disturbs the quietude of that pool of silence which we call the air, it ripples into overtones, which, becoming fainter and fainter, die away into silence. It would seem reasonable to assume that the combination of numbers which express these overtones, if translated into terms of space, would yield proportions agreeable to the eye, and such is the fact, as the accompanying examples sufficiently indicate (Illustrations 88-91).

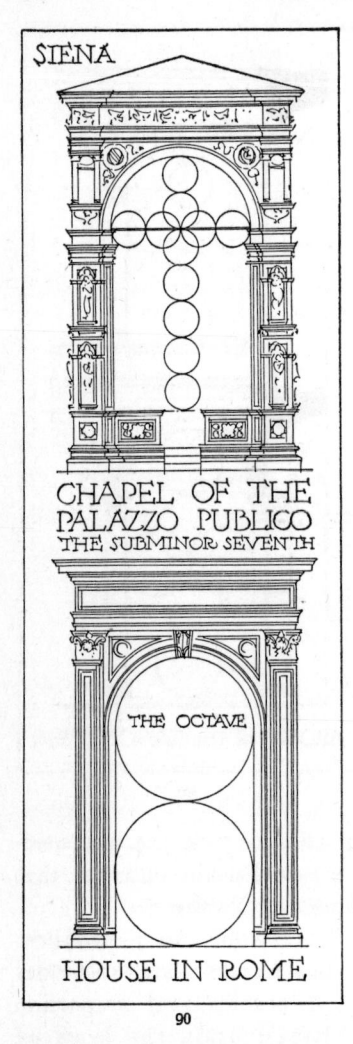

The interval of the sub-minor seventh (4:7), used in this way, in connection with the simpler intervals of the octave (1:2), and the fifth (2:3), is particularly pleasing because it is neither too obvious nor too subtle. This ratio of 4:7 is important for the reason that it expresses the angle of sixty degrees, that is, the numbers 4 and 7 represent (very nearly) the ratio between one-half the base and the altitude of an equilateral triangle; also because they form part of the numerical series 1, 4, 7, 10, etc. Both are "mystic" numbers, and in Gothic architecture, particularly, proportions were frequently determined by numbers to which a mystic value was attached. According to Gwilt, the Gothic chapels of Windsor and Oxford are divided longitudinally by four, and transversely by seven equal parts. The arcade above the roses in the façade of the cathedral of Tours shows seven principal units across the front of the nave, and four in each of the towers.

A distinguishing characteristic of the series of ratios which represent the consonant intervals within the compass of an octave is that it advances by the addition of 1 to both terms: 1:2, 2:3, 3:4, 4:5, and 5:6. Such a

VII FROZEN MUSIC 89

series always approaches unity, just as, represented graphically by means of parallelograms, it tends towards a square. According to W. Watkins Lloyd—in an article published in The American Architect of March 31, 1888—the scale of ratios which determined all the important proportions of the Parthenon is of this order, advancing by consecutive differences of 5. The author has no means of verifying the truth of this statement, but gives it here for what it is worth (Illustration 92). Alberti in his book presents a design for a tower showing his idea for its general proportions. It consists of six stories, in a sequence of orders. The lowest story is a perfect cube and each of the other stories is 11-12 of the story below, or diminishing practically in the proportion of 8, 7, 6, 5, 4, 3, allowing in each case for the amount hidden by the projection of the cornice below; each order being accurate as regards column, entablature, etc. It is of interest to compare this with Ruskin's idea in his "Seven Lamps," where he takes the case of a plant called Alisma Plantago, in which the various branches diminish in the proportion of 7, 6, 5, 4, 3, respectively, and so carry out the same idea; on which Ruskin observes that diminution in a building should be after the manner of Nature.

ARCADE of the CANCELLERIA
91

GRAPHICAL EXPRESSION OF MUSICAL INTERVALS.

SCALE SHOWING PRINCIPAL PROPORTIONS OF THE PARTHENON.

92

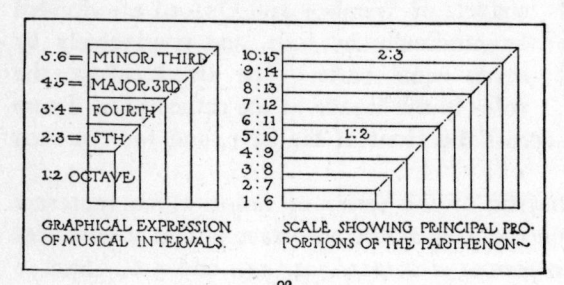

It would be a profitless task to formulate exact rules of architectural proportion based upon the laws of musical harmony. The two arts are too different from each other for that, and moreover the last appeal must always be to the eye,

THE PALAZZO VERZI AT VERONA (LOWER PORTION ONLY). A COMPOSITION FOUNDED ON THE EQUAL AND REGULAR DIVISION OF SPACE, AS MUSIC IS FOUNDED ON THE EQUAL AND REGULAR DIVISION OF TIME

93

ARCHITECTURE AS RHYTHM A DIVISION OF SPACE CORRESPONDING TO 3/4 AND 4/4 TIME

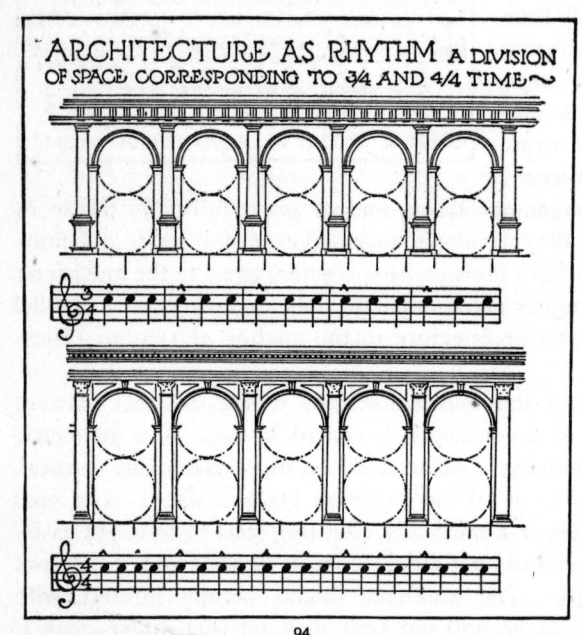

94

and not to a mathematical formula, just as in music the last appeal is to the ear. Laws there are, but they discover themselves to the artist as he proceeds, and are for the most part incommunicable. Rules and formulas are useful and valuable not as a substitute for inspiration, but as a guide: not as wings, but as a tail. In this connection perhaps all that is necessary for the architectural designer to bear in mind is that important ratios of length and breadth, height and and width, to be "musical" should be expressed by quantitatively small numbers, and that if possible they should obey some simple law of numerical progression. From this basic simplicity complexity will follow, but it will be an ordered and harmonious complexity, like that of a tree, or of a symphony.

In the same way that a musical composition implies the division of time into equal and regular beats, so a work of architecture should have for its basis some unit of space. This unit should be nowhere too obvious and may be varied within certain limits, just as musical time is retarded or accelerated. The underlying rhythm and symmetry will thus give value and distinction to such variation. Vasari tells how Brunelleschi, Bramante and Leonardo da Vinci used to work on paper ruled in squares, describing it as a "truly ingenious thing, and of great utility in the work of design." By this means they developed proportions according to a definite scheme. They set to work with a division of space analogous to the musician's division of time. The examples given herewith indicate how close a parallel may exist between music and architecture in this matter of ryhthm (Illustrations 93-95).

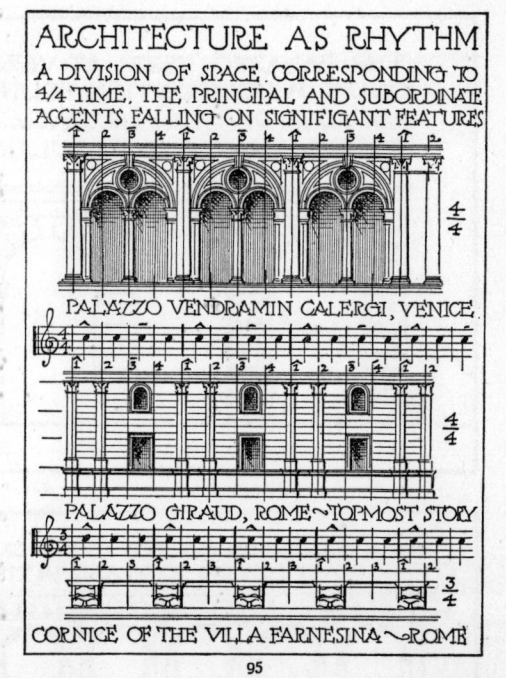

It is a demonstrable fact that musical sounds weave invisible patterns in the air. Architecture, correspondingly, in one of its aspects, is geometric pattern made fixed and enduring. What could be more essentially musical, for example, than the sea arcade of the Venetian Ducal Palace? The sand forms traced by sound-waves on a musically vibrating steel plate might easily suggest architectural ornament did not the differences of scale and of material tend to confuse the mind. The architect should occupy himself with identities, not differences. If he will but bear in mind that architecture is pattern in space, just as music is pattern in time, he will come to perceive the essential identity between, say a Greek rosette and a Gothic rose-window;

an arcade and an egg and dart moulding (Illustration 96). All architectural forms and arrangements which give enduring pleasure are in their essence musical. Every well composed façade makes harmony in three dimensions; every good roof line sings a melody against the sky.

CONCLUSION

IN taking leave of the reader at the end of this excursion together among the by-ways of a beautiful art, the author must needs add a final word or two touching upon the purpose and scope of these essays. Architecture (like everything else) has two aspects: it may be viewed from the standpoint of utility, that is, as construction: or from the standpoint of expressiveness, that is, as decoration. No attempt has been made here to deal with its first aspect, and of the second (which is again two-fold) only the universal, not the particular expressiveness has been sought. The literature of architecture is rich in works dealing with the utilitarian and constructive side of the art: indeed, it may be said that to this side that literature is almost exclusively devoted. This being so, it has seemed worth while to attempt to show the obverse of the medal, even though it be "tails" instead of "heads."

One possible criticism the author meets, not with apologies, but with defiance. The inductive method has not, in these pages, been honored by a due observance. It would have been easy to have treated the subject inductively, amassing facts and drawing conclusions, but to have done so the author would have been false to the very principle about which the work came into being. With the acceptance of the Ancient Wisdom, the inductive method becomes a thing of the past. Facts are no longer useful in order to establish a hypothesis, they are used rather to elucidate a known and accepted truth; and when theosophy shall have become the universal religion of mankind, this work, if it survives at all, will be chiefly, perhaps solely, remarkable by reason of the fact that it was among the first in which the attempt was made to again unify science, art, and religion, as they were unified in those ancient times and among those ancient peoples when the Wisdom swayed the hearts and minds of men.